American Medical Association
Physicians dedicated to the health of America

cpt® Coding Workbook

Coding Challenges and Exercises for Instructors and Students

EDITED BY
Catherine Duffy, BS, RHIT

AMA press

cpt® Coding Workbook

Coding Challenges and Exercises for Instructors and Students

For information regarding the reprinting or licensing, or parts hereof, of *CPT® Coding Workbook: Coding Challenges and Exercises for Instructors and Students*, please contact:

CPT Intellectual Property Services
American Medical Association
515 North State Street
Chicago, Illinois 60610
312 464-5022

Additional copies of this book may be ordered by calling 800 621-8335 or from the secure AMA Press Web site at www.amapress.com. Refer to product number OP570404.

ISBN 1-57947-424-1
AC24:04-P-080:12/04

Cover illustration ©Ketler/SIS.

Contents

Preface

Coders, students, and instructors often ask for more practical, real-life coding studies with rationales to help ensure accurate interpretation of the Current Procedural Terminology (CPT®) code set. The American Medical Association has produced several CPT educational products, including *Principles of CPT® Coding*, and decided that a coding workbook with additional study material may help to fill this need.

Written by the AMA's CPT coding experts in a joint effort with the CPT advisors from various specialty societies, the *CPT® Coding Workbook: Coding Challenges and Exercises for Instructors and Students* addresses introductory to intermediate coding skills by incorporating basic and moderately difficult coding scenarios and operative procedures with the appropriate code assignment. The *Coding Workbook* is appropriate to use in conjunction with the CPT codebook and *Principles of CPT® Coding* or on its own; however, combining study of *Principles of CPT® Coding* with the *Coding Workbook* can make learning to code easier.

The *Coding Workbook* is designed to be used by community colleges, career colleges, and vocational school programs for training coders, medical assistants, medical insurance specialists, and other healthcare providers. It can also be used as an independent study training tool for new medical office personnel, physicians, independent billing services personnel, and others in the healthcare field who want to learn additional coding skills.

In the *Coding Workbook* you will find:

- Information about the CPT coding format and conventions
- Clarification of the CPT coding guidelines and their application with coding questions and operative procedures (topics covered include E/M, anesthesiology, surgery, radiology, and medicine)
- Exercises at the end of each chapter in several formats: true/false, multiple choice, and scenario reporting
- An extensive answer key with rationales conveniently located in the back of the book with perforated pages for easy removal
- Coding tips scattered throughout that provide even more help in assigning the correct code

When reading and using the *Coding Workbook* you must always keep in mind that the information presented is from the CPT coding perspective and conveys the CPT Editorial Panel's intent behind various codes. Payment policies are set by third-party payers and not by CPT staff. Therefore, any specific payment-related questions or issues must be directed to the respective third-party payer.

About the Editor

Catherine Duffy, BS, RHIT, is the Director of CPT® Information and Education Services for the American Medical Association (AMA) and has 25 years' experience in health information technology and management. Catherine's primary responsibilities include managing the CPT Information Services (CPT-IS) department and serving as the technical editor for *CPT® Assistant* and *Clinical Examples* newsletters. She assists in the publication of *CPT® Changes: An Insider's View*, *Principles of CPT® Coding*, and the CPT codebook. Prior to her position as Director of CPT-Information and Education Services, she was involved with the CPT-5 Project.

Catherine has held a variety of positions in other healthcare organizations such as director in a health information department, CPT coding educator for a health information technology program, and coding consultant for physicians' offices. Catherine has also served in several coding and transcription positions and has provided CPT coding education through nationwide presentations. Catherine is a member of the curricula advisory committee for the Health Information Technology program at the College of Lake County in Grayslake, Illinois.

Catherine holds an Associate of Applied Science in Health Information Technology from the College of Lake County, a Bachelor of Science degree in Healthcare Management from Southern Illinois University, and completed a pre-medicine program at the College of Lake County. She is a member of the American Health Information Management Association and the Illinois Health Information Management Association.

Acknowledgments

We would like to express sincere gratitude to the CPT® advisors and their staff from the following specialty societies who submitted and reviewed coding scenarios for this workbook:

American Academy of Allergy, Asthma, and Immunology
American Academy of Dermatology Association
American Academy of Family Physicians
American Academy of Neurology
American Academy of Pediatrics
American Academy of Physical Medicine and Rehabilitation
American Clinical Neurophysiology Society
American College of Allergy, Asthma, and Immunology
American College of Emergency Physicians
American College of Gastroenterology
American College of Obstetrics and Gynecologists
American College of Radiation Oncology
American College of Radiology
American College of Rheumatology
American Dietetic Association
American Gastroenterological Association
American Optometric Association
American Physical Therapy Association
American Podiatric Medical Association
American Psychological Association
American Society for Dermatologic Surgery
American Society for Gastrointestinal Endoscopy
American Society of Anesthesiologists
American Society of Cataract and Refractive Surgery
American Society of Clinical Oncology
American Urological Association
Society of American Gastrointestinal Endoscopic Surgeons
Society of Interventional Radiology
Society of Nuclear Medicine

We would also like to thank the efforts of the entire AMA CPT Editorial Information Services staff, most notably, Michael Beebe, Director of CPT Editorial and Information Services; Marie Mindeman, Director of CPT

Editorial Research and Development; and Karen O'Hara, Senior Coding Consultant. We would also like to thank Laurie Desjardins, CPC and Judy Breuker, CPC, CCS-P, CHCC, CHBME, the consultants who reviewed each chapter. Their comments and suggestions were helpful in completing this book. Others who contributed to the publication of this book include:

Jean Roberts, Director, Production and Manufacturing
Elise Schumacher, Senior Acquisitions Editor
Katharine Dvorak, Developmental Editor
Amy Postlewait, Marketing Manager
Rosalyn Carlton, Senior Production Coordinator
Ronnie Summers, Senior Print Coordinator

Introduction to CPT® Coding

Basics of the CPT Codebook

Learning the CPT coding system and nomenclature can be overwhelming. Therefore, it is important to have a solid foundation on which to build your CPT coding knowledge. An essential building block in this foundation is having a thorough understanding of medical terminology and anatomy in order to code correctly. The intention of this introduction is to guide you through the basics of CPT coding and jumpstart your knowledge base.

To begin, become acquainted with the CPT codebook's layout, section numbers, and sequences. Next, look at the various code symbols that appear throughout the book. Learn about the format of the terminology in CPT coding. Taking the time to review basic CPT coding concepts will help you develop that solid foundation you will need for assigning CPT codes as well as give you the tools to address the coding exercises in this workbook.

There are eight sections in the CPT codebook. The first six sections, which pertain to Category I CPT codes, include:

- Evaluation and Management (E/M)
- Anesthesiology
- Surgery
- Radiology
- Pathology and Laboratory
- Medicine

The seventh and eighth sections pertain to the Category II performance measurement CPT codes and the Category III new/emerging technology codes, respectively.

The procedures and services listed in the CPT nomenclature are presented in numeric order, with the exception of the E/M section, which appears at the beginning of the book. (Because these codes are used by most physicians in reporting a significant portion of their services, they were placed at the front of the book for easy reference.)

Instructions for Reporting Medical Services and Procedures

When procedures and services by a physician are reported, the CPT code that most accurately identifies the service performed should be selected. Any service or procedure reported should be adequately documented in the medical record to support the specific code(s) reported. Do not select a CPT code that merely approximates the service provided. If no such procedure or service exists in the CPT code set, then report the service by using the appropriate Unlisted Procedure or Service code. Some people maintain that they are discouraged from using Unlisted Procedure codes or not allowed to use them altogether. While the use of an Unlisted Procedure or Service code will require a special report or documentation to describe the service, correct coding demands that a "square peg" not be fit into a "round hole."

Placement of a Code in the CPT Code Set

When procedures and services are evaluated for reimbursement or other purposes, it is important to consider each procedure and service on its own merits, and not simply on the placement of the code in the CPT nomenclature. The listing of a procedure or service in a specific section of the CPT codebook does not restrict its use to a specific specialty group. Any procedure or service in any section of the book may be used to designate the services rendered by any qualified physician or other health care professional.

Because the CPT nomenclature is not a strict classification system, there may be some procedures that appear in sections other than in those where they might ordinarily be "classified." From a historical perspective, CPT coding has always placed procedures in general sections according to where physicians will most conveniently find them.

EXAMPLE

The code for a diagnostic colonoscopy, although not involving an incision, is located in the Digestive System subsection. This was done because keeping the endoscopies involving a biopsy, tumor removal, or other operative intervention in proximity to the diagnostic procedure was considered important.

EXAMPLE

Cast applications are listed in the Musculoskeletal subsection in proximity to the fracture and dislocation treatments; however, a cast application is not a "surgical" procedure.

Format of the Terminology

Without developing a basic understanding of the format of the terminology in CPT coding, appropriate use of the CPT codebook would be almost impossible. Understanding how to read the full description of the CPT codes is a necessary and fundamental concept to learn and will assist you in appropriate use of the CPT codebook.

The format of the terminology was originally developed as stand-alone descriptions of medical procedures. However, to conserve space and avoid having to repeat common terminology, some of the procedure descriptors in CPT coding are not printed in their entirety, but rather refer back to a common portion of the procedure descriptor listed in a preceding entry. Within any indented series of codes, you must refer back to the first left-justified code (parent code) within that series to determine the full procedure descriptor of the indented code(s) that follows.

EXAMPLE

97010 Application of a modality to one or more areas; hot or cold packs

97012 traction, mechanical

97014 electrical stimulation (unattended)

97016 vasopneumatic devices

The common part of the parent code, **97010** (that part of the description to the left of the semicolon, "Application of a modality to one or more areas;"), should be considered part of each of the following indented codes in that series (**97012–97028**).

The full procedure descriptor represented by code **97012** actually reads:

97012 Application of a modality to one or more areas; traction, mechanical

Simply because a code is indented within a series does not mean that one code from a series cannot be reported with another code within the same indented series. If two distinct procedures are performed, then both procedures can be reported. However, in such a case, the use of CPT modifiers becomes necessary. (See "Modifiers" later in this introduction for more information about using CPT modifiers.)

Code Symbols

Over the years, a number of code symbols have been incorporated into the CPT codebook to make CPT nomenclature user-friendly. It is important to know these symbols:

● Whenever new procedure codes are added to the CPT code set, they are identified throughout the CPT codebook with the bullet symbol preceding the code number. Note that this symbol appears for only one year, the year the code is added.

▲ The triangle is used to designate codes with a substantially altered description. Once again, this symbol appears for only one year, the year the code is revised.

▶◀ Sideways triangles are used throughout the CPT codebook to indicate new and revised text, such as new parenthetical notes and language added to guidelines. They do not apply to code descriptors (see ▲). These symbols appear for only one year, the year the new and revised text is added.

✚ Add-on codes (a special category of CPT codes) are identified with the plus symbol preceding the codes. This symbol was introduced in 1999. Add-on codes can also be identified by specific language in the code descriptor, such as "each additional" or "(List separately in addition to primary procedure)." A complete list of all add-on codes in the CPT code set can be found in Appendix D in the CPT codebook.

⊘ This symbol designates CPT codes that are exempt from the use of modifier 51, but have not been designated as CPT add-on procedures/services. As an added reference, Appendix E in the CPT codebook also contains a complete list of the codes exempt from modifier 51 usage.

➲ The arrow symbol indicates that the American Medical Association has published reference material in *CPT® Changes: An Insider's View* or in *CPT® Assistant* newsletter on that particular code. *CPT Changes* is published annually and includes educational instruction related to new, revised, and deleted codes. *CPT Assistant* is the AMA's monthly authoritative coding newsletter that contains educational instruction related to new, revised, or deleted codes.

⊙ This symbol, introduced in 2005, is used to identify the CPT codes that include conscious sedation, which are listed in Appendix G in the CPT codebook.

EXAMPLE

An entry that reads ➲ CPT Assistant Feb 96:4 and appears after a specific code descriptor indicates that information regarding that code can be found in the February 1996 issue of *CPT Assistant* newsletter on page 4.

Guidelines

Specific guidelines for reporting procedures and services can be found at the beginning of each of the six sections of the CPT codebook. These guidelines provide information that is necessary to appropriately interpret and report the procedures and services with the CPT codes found in that section.

In addition to the guidelines that appear at the beginning of each section, several of the subheadings or subsections have special instructions that are unique to that section. These types of guidelines and instructional notes appear throughout the CPT codebook (eg, at the beginning of a category or subcategory of codes and in parenthetical notes either preceding or following a code). All of the guidelines and notes in the CPT codebook are there to assist users of the CPT nomenclature in appropriate interpretation and application of the codes throughout the book. These guidelines and notes are critical to using CPT codes correctly. Many of these guidelines can be found in the chapters of this workbook as instructional notes.

Modifiers

CPT nomenclature uses modifiers as an integral part of its structure. Modifiers are appended to CPT codes to indicate that a performed service or procedure has been altered or modified by some specific circumstance, but not changed in its definition. Appending the appropriate modifier can be crucial for reimbursement when a CPT code is reported in a specific circumstance. CPT modifiers are two-digit numeric indicators. Appendix A of the CPT codebook contains a complete listing of these modifiers and their definitions. For CPT 2004, hyphens were removed that previously appeared before the modifier numbers. This revision continues throughout the CPT nomenclature in 2005. (For more information about modifiers, refer to *Coding with Modifiers: A Guide to Correct CPT® and HCPCS Level II Modifier Usage*, published by AMA Press.)

Appendixes

There are nine appendixes located in the back of the CPT codebook:

- Appendix A includes a complete list of the CPT modifiers and their definitions.
- Appendix B includes a summary of additions, deletions, and revisions.
- Appendix C includes clinical examples for E/M codes.
- Appendix D includes a summary of CPT add-on codes. These codes are also identified throughout the text of the CPT codebook with the ✚ symbol placed before the code.
- Appendix E includes a summary of CPT codes that are exempt from the use of modifier 51. These codes, however, are not designated as CPT add-on codes. They are identified throughout the text of the CPT codebook with the ⊘ symbol placed before the code.
- Appendix F includes a summary of the CPT codes that are exempt from the use of modifier 63.
- Appendix G includes a summary of the CPT codes that include conscious sedation.
- Appendix H is an alphabetic index of performance measures by clinical condition or topic.
- Appendix I includes a list of the genetic testing code modifiers.

Appendixes F–I were added to the CPT codebook in 2005.

Alphabetic Index

The index is located after the appendixes in the CPT codebook. It is important to note that the alphabetic index is *not* a substitute for the main text of the CPT nomenclature. Even if only one code appears in the index, the user must refer to the main text of the CPT codebook to ensure that the code selection is accurate.

The index is organized by main terms. There are four primary classes of main index entries:

- **Procedure or service** (for example, Allergen Immunotherapy, Arthroscopy, Biopsy, Cardiac Catheterization, Debridement, Evaluation and Management, Laparoscopy, Osteopathic Manipulation, Physical Medicine/Therapy/Occupational Therapy, Vaccines)
- **Organ or other anatomic site** (for example, Abdomen, Bladder, Esophagus, Hip, Intestines, Malar Area, Olecranon Process, Prostate)
- **Condition** (for example, Abscess, Blepharoptosis, Dislocation, Esophageal Varices, Hemorrhage, Omphalocele, Varicose Vein)
- **Synonyms, eponyms, and abbreviations** (for example, Anderson Tibial Lengthening, CBC, Clagett Procedure, EKG, Patterson's Test)

A main term may be followed by a series of up to three indented terms that modify the main term. These modifying terms should be reviewed, as these sub-terms have an effect on appropriate code selection.

Cross-references provide additional instructions to the user. There are two types of cross-references in the index:

- ***See***. This type of reference is used primarily for synonyms, eponyms, and abbreviations. As an added reference, a list of common abbreviations can be found on the back cover of the professional edition of the CPT codebook and inside the back cover of the standard edition.
- ***See Also***. This reference directs the user to look under another main term if the procedure is not listed under the first main index entry.

Reviewing and understanding the basics of CPT coding is an important first step into this workbook. The next step in becoming a more effect coder is the application of these basics to each chapter of the CPT codebook.

CHAPTER 1

Evaluation and Management Services

OBJECTIVES

This chapter will assist in accomplishing the following objectives:

- Understand the basic format of levels of Evaluation and Management (E/M) services
- Understand the key words, phrases, and definitions that pertain to E/M services
- Understand the Instructions for Selecting a Level of E/M
- Understand the guidelines for E/M categories

Introduction to Evaluation and Management Services

The Evaluation and Management (E/M) services codes were introduced into the Current Procedural Terminology (CPT®) nomenclature in 1992. These codes describe services provided by physicians to evaluate patients and manage their care. The E/M codes replaced "visit" codes that described services in general terms such as a brief, intermediate, or comprehensive visit, for example. The E/M codes are widely used by physicians of all specialties and describe a large portion of the medical care provided to patients of all ages. The basic format of the levels of E/M services is the same for most categories:

- Place and/or type of service
- Content of service defined
- Nature of presenting problem associated with a given level
- Time typically required to provide the service

E/M codes are divided into the following categories and subcategories:

- Office or Other Outpatient Services
    - New Patient **99201–99205**
    - Established Patient **99211–99215**
- Hospital Observation Services
    - Observation Care Discharge Services **99217**
    - Initial Observation Care **99218–99220**
- Hospital Inpatient Services
    - Initial Hospital Care **99221–99223**
    - Subsequent Hospital Care **99231–99233**
    - Hospital Discharge Services **99238–99239**
- Consultations
    - Office or Other Outpatient Consultations **99241–99245**
    - Initial Inpatient Consultations **99251–99255**
    - Follow-up Inpatient Consultations **99261–99263**
    - Confirmatory Consultations **99271–99275**
- Emergency Department Services **99281–99288**
- Pediatric Critical Care Patient Transport **99289–99290**
- Critical Care Services **99291–99292**
- Inpatient Pediatric Critical Care **99293–99294**
- Inpatient Neonatal Critical Care **99295–99296**
- Intensive (Non-Critical) Low Birth Weight Services **99298–99299**
- Nursing Facility Services
    - Comprehensive Nursing Facility Assessments **99301–99303**
    - Subsequent Nursing Facility Care **99311–99313**
    - Nursing Facility Discharge Services **99315–99316**
- Domiciliary, Rest Home (eg, Boarding Home), or Custodial Care Services
    - New Patient **99321–99323**
    - Established Patient **99331–99333**
- Home Services
    - New Patient **99341–99345**
    - Established Patient **99347–99350**

- Prolonged Services
  - Prolonged Physician Service With Direct (Face-to-Face) Patient Contact **99354–99357**
  - Prolonged Physician Service Without Direct (Face-to-Face) Patient Contact **99358–99359**
  - Physician Standby Services **99360**
- Case Management Services
  - Team Conferences **99361–99362**
  - Telephone Calls **99371–99373**
- Care Plan Oversight Services **99374–99380**
- Preventive Medicine Services
  - New Patient **99381–99387**
  - Established Patient **99391–99397**
  - Preventive Medicine, Individual Counseling **99401–99404**
  - Preventive Medicine, Group Counseling **99411–99412**
  - Other Preventive Medicine Services **99420–99429**
- Newborn Care **99431–99440**
- Special Evaluation and Management Services
  - Basic Life and/or Disability Evaluation Services **99450**
  - Work Related or Medical Disability Evaluation Services . . **99455–99456**
- Other Evaluation and Management Services **99499**

New and Established Patients

Many of the E/M services CPT codes differentiate between new and established patients. A *new patient* is one who has not received any professional services from the physician or another physician of the same specialty who belongs to the same group practice within the past three years. An *established patient* is one who has received professional services from the physician or another physician of the same specialty who belongs to the same group practice within the past three years. When a physician is on call for or covering for another physician, the patient's encounter is classified as it would have been by the physician who is not available. No distinction is made between new and established patients in the emergency department. E/M services in the Emergency Department Services category may be reported for any new or established patient who presents for treatment in the emergency department.

Levels of E/M Services

Within each category or subcategory of E/M services, there are three to five levels of E/M services available for reporting purposes. Levels of E/M services are not interchangeable among the different categories or subcategories of service. The descriptors for the levels of E/M services recognize seven components, six of which are used in defining the levels of E/M services. These components are:

- History
- Examination
- Medical decision making

- Counseling
- Coordination of care
- Nature of presenting problem
- Time

The first three of these components (history, examination, and medical decision making) are considered the key components in selecting a level of E/M services. As a general rule, these are the first components considered when the level of E/M service to report is determined. However, as with most rules, there are exceptions, eg, in the case of visits that consist primarily of counseling or coordination of care.

Selecting the Appropriate Level of E/M Services

E/M services are selected on the basis of either the key components or time. For the following categories/subcategories, *all three* of the key components (ie, history, examination, and medical decision making) must meet or exceed the stated requirements to qualify for a particular level of E/M service: office, new patient; hospital observation services; initial hospital care; office consultations; initial inpatient consultations; confirmatory consultations; emergency department services; comprehensive nursing facility assessments; domiciliary care, new patient; and home, new patient.

For the following categories/subcategories, *two* of the three key components (ie, history, examination, and medical decision making) must meet or exceed the stated requirements to qualify for a particular level of E/M services: office, established patient; subsequent hospital care; follow-up inpatient consultations; subsequent nursing facility care; domiciliary care, established patient; and home, established patient.

When counseling and/or coordination of care dominate (more than 50%) the physician/patient and/or family encounter (face-to-face time in the office or other outpatient setting or floor/unit time in the hospital or nursing facility), then time may be considered the key or controlling factor to qualify for selecting a particular level of E/M services. This includes time spent with parties who have assumed responsibility for the care of the patient or decision making, whether or not they are family members (eg, foster parents, person acting in locum parentis, legal guardian). The extent of counseling and/or coordination of care must be documented in the medical record.

Specific guidelines are also included in the categories and subcategories of the E/M services codes. It is important to also review these guidelines when selecting an appropriate E/M service code.

Office or Other Outpatient Services

The Office or Other Outpatient Services codes (**99201–99215**) are used to report E/M services provided in the physician's office or other outpatient/ambulatory settings, including E/M services provided in an urgent care setting. Office and Other Outpatient Services include the subcategories of new and established patient visits. When new patient visits are reported, all three key components must meet or exceed the stated requirements to qualify for a particular level of E/M service. When established patient visits are reported, two of the three key components must meet or exceed the stated requirements to qualify for a particular level of E/M service.

If a patient is admitted to the hospital in the course of the office encounter, all E/M services provided by the physician in conjunction with the admission are considered part of the initial hospital care, when performed on the same date as the admission. A separate code for the office visit is not reported. The initial hospital care level of service reported by the admitting physician should include the services related to the admission provided in the physician's office, as well as the E/M services the physician provided on that same date in the inpatient setting.

Hospital Observation Services

Hospital Observation Services codes (**99217–99220**) are used to report E/M services provided to patients designated or admitted as "observation status" in a hospital. These patients are there to be observed to determine whether they should be admitted to the hospital, transferred to another facility, or sent home. Since not all hospitals have a specific area designated for observation patients, the patient does not have to be located in an observation area designated by the hospital. Instead, the patient can be designated or admitted as observation status in the medical record. Codes in this category are *not* used to report hospital observation services involving admission and discharge services provided on the same date. Hospital Observation or Inpatient Care Services involving admission and discharge services provided on the same date are reported with codes **99234–99236**.

Codes **99218–99220** are used to report the initial observation care and are reported for new or established patient visits. When these codes are reported, it is necessary for all three of the key components to meet or exceed the requirements stated in the code descriptor to qualify for a particular level of service. Code **99217** is used to report observation care discharge day management. This code is used by the physician to report final examination of the patient, discussion of the observation stay, instructions for continuing care, and preparation of discharge records. This code is reported only if the discharge from observation status is on a date other than the initial date of observation status. In the event that an observation stay exceeds two days, the appropriate initial observation care code is reported for the initial day, code **99217** is reported for the observation care discharge day, and code **99499**, Unlisted Evaluation and Management Service, is reported for the observation days in between the initial day and the discharge day.

If the physician provides an E/M service on a given date in another site (eg, physician's office, hospital emergency department, nursing facility) and subsequently initiates observation status in a hospital for that patient on the same date, the physician reports only an initial observation care code for all E/M services provided on that date. The level of initial observation care reported by the supervising physician should include the services provided in the other site of service as well as those provided in the observation setting. If a patient is designated as observation status on a given date and is subsequently admitted to the hospital on that date, only an initial hospital care code is reported for both of these E/M services provided on that date. The initial hospital care level of service reported should include all E/M services provided on that date.

The hospital observation codes are not intended to be used to report physician services related to postoperative recovery of a patient. No E/M code is reported for E/M services provided by the physician who performs a surgery and then routinely evaluates the patient in an observation area postoperatively. The global surgical package generally includes those evaluations immediately after surgery.

Hospital Inpatient Services

The Hospital Inpatient Services codes (**99221–99239**) are used to report E/M services provided to hospital inpatients. Services include three subcategories of codes: Initial Hospital Care, Subsequent Hospital Care, and Hospital Discharge Services. Patients in a partial hospital setting are also included in this range of codes. A partial hospital setting is used for crisis stabilization, intensive short-term daily treatment, or intermediate-term treatment of psychiatric disorders.

Initial Hospital Care

Initial Hospital Care codes (**99221–99223**) are used to report new or established patient E/M services. These codes are intended to be reported for the first hospital inpatient encounter by the admitting physician. This date may not be the same as the date the patient was actually admitted to the hospital.

EXAMPLE

The physician provided an E/M service to the patient in the office on Wednesday and subsequently admitted the patient to the hospital on that same day. However, the physician did not have an inpatient encounter with that patient until Thursday morning. In this scenario, the appropriate code for office or other outpatient level of E/M service is reported for the E/M services provided on Wednesday. The date of service and appropriate code for the initial hospital care will be Thursday's date—the date the admitting physician had the first hospital inpatient encounter with the patient.

The initial hospital care level of service reported by the admitting physician should include all E/M services provided to that patient in conjunction with that admission on the same date. For example, if the physician provides an E/M service to the patient in the office (or other site of service) on Wednesday, admits the patient to the hospital, and subsequently has an inpatient encounter with that patient all on the same date (Wednesday), then the initial hospital care level of service reported should include all E/M services provided on that date.

A separate code would not be reported for the E/M services provided in the office (or other site of service) on that date.

The initial hospital care level of service codes include all E/M services provided to that patient in conjunction with that admission on the same date. A separate code would not be reported for the E/M services provided in the office (or other site of service) on that same date.

Subsequent Hospital Care

Subsequent Hospital Care codes (**99231–99233**) are reported to identify services provided by the admitting physician on dates subsequent to the provision of initial hospital care. When subsequent hospital care is reported, at least two of the three key components must meet or exceed the stated requirements to qualify for a particular level of E/M service.

Hospital Discharge Services

The Hospital Discharge Services codes (**99238** and **99239**) are reported for the total time spent by the attending physician for hospital discharge of the patient provided the date of discharge is different from the date of admission. These codes include final examination of the patient, discussion of the hospital stay, instructions for continuing care to all relevant caregivers, and preparation of discharge records, prescriptions, and referral forms. The Hospital Discharge Services codes may be used to report discharge services provided to patients who die during the hospital stay.

Consultations

A *consultation* is defined as a type of service provided by a physician whose opinion or advice regarding evaluation and/or management of a specific problem is requested by another physician or other appropriate source. Types of consultations include the following:

- Office or Other Outpatient Consultations
- Initial Inpatient Consultations
- Follow-up Inpatient Consultations

A consultation must include the following elements:

- A written or verbal request for a consultation, made by a physician or other appropriate source, must be documented in the patient's medical record.
- The consultant must document his or her opinion and any services ordered or performed.
- The consultant may initiate diagnostic and/or therapeutic services at the same or a subsequent visit.
- The consultant must communicate, in a written report, the opinion and any services ordered or performed to the requesting physician or other appropriate source.

Office or Other Outpatient Consultations

The Office or Other Outpatient Consultations codes (**99241–99245**) are used to report consultations provided in the office or other outpatient setting, including the physician's office; a hospital observation service; home services; domiciliary, rest home, or custodial care; emergency department; or other ambulatory facility. There is no differentiation between new and established patient visits. When the codes in this subcategory of service are reported, all three key components must meet or exceed the stated requirements to qualify for a particular level of service.

Follow-up visits provided in the consultant's office or other outpatient facility that are initiated by the consulting physician are reported by using codes in the Office or Other Outpatient Services category for established patient visits (**99211–99215**).

Initial Inpatient Consultations

The Initial Inpatient Consultations codes (**99251–99255**) are used to report consultations provided to hospital inpatients or residents of nursing facilities. Within this series of codes there is no differentiation between new and established patient visits. When the codes in this subcategory are reported, all three key components must meet or exceed the requirements of the code descriptor to qualify for a particular level of service. Only one initial inpatient consultation per admission should be reported by a consultant for a particular patient.

Follow-up Inpatient Consultations

The Follow-up Inpatient Consultations codes (**99261–99263**) are used to report follow-up consultations provided to hospital inpatients or nursing facility residents only. For consultations provided in other settings, the codes for Office or Other Outpatient Consultations (**99241–99245**) should be reported. When the codes in this subcategory of service are reported, two of the three key components must meet or exceed the requirements of the code descriptor to qualify for a particular level of service. Follow-up inpatient consultations are visits scheduled to complete the initial consultation and are initiated by the consultant for subsequent consultative visits. If the consultant is unable to finish the initial consultation because, for example, certain test results are not available, then the physician consultant may visit the patient on a date subsequent to the initial consultative visit to complete the initial consultation. The consultant selects the follow-up inpatient consultation code for the services he or she has performed in this subsequent consultative visit. The documentation in the patient's medical record must indicate the consultant's opinion or advice.

Consultation vs referral

From a CPT coding perspective, the terms *consultation* and *referral* are not used interchangeably. When a physician refers a patient to another physician, it is not automatically a consultation. A consultation would be appropriate if the E/M service provided meets the above criteria for reporting a consultation. If a physician sends a patient to another physician for specialized care, which is not in his or her domain, and the physician to whom the patient is referred does not communicate his or her opinion or advice to the requesting physician, then this is not a consultation.

Confirmatory Consultations

Confirmatory Consultations codes (**99271–99275**) are reported when an opinion is sought for confirmatory purposes. The physician consultant providing a confirmatory consultation is expected to provide only an opinion and/or advice during the first evaluation, unless minor diagnostic procedures (eg, anoscopy to advise about hemorrhoid treatment) are a key requirement to provide the opinion.

Emergency Department Services

An *emergency department* is defined as an organized hospital-based facility for the provision of unscheduled episodic services to patients who present for immediate medical attention. E/M services provided in the emergency department, regardless of whether the patient is new or established, are reported with the codes in this series (**99281–99285**). When the codes in this category of service are reported, all three key components must be met. These codes are not limited to use by emergency department physicians. Time is not a descriptive component for emergency department levels of service because they are typically provided on a variable-intensity basis, often involving multiple encounters over an extended period. The descriptor of code **99285** is differentiated in that it indicates that three key components are required "within the constraints imposed by the urgency of the patient's clinical condition and/or mental status." This allows code **99285** to be reported even if the patient's condition precludes the completion of the comprehensive history and/or the comprehensive examination. Code **99285** can also be reported when the patient's condition normally requires this level of service, but the physician is unable to complete a comprehensive-level history or examination.

Pediatric Patient Transport Services

The Pediatric Patient Transport Services codes (**99289** and **99290**) are time-based codes reported for pediatric patients (24 months of age or less) who are critically ill or injured, who receive face-to-face critical care services delivered by a physician during interfacility transport. Only the time the physician spends in direct face-to-face contact with the patient during the transport should be reported. Pediatric patient transport services involving less than 30 minutes of face-to-face physician care should not be reported with codes **99289** and **99290**. Procedure(s) or service(s) performed by other members of the transporting team may not be reported by the supervising physician.

Critical Care Services

The Critical Care Services codes (**99291** and **99292**) are time-based codes for reporting the total duration of time on a given date spent by a physician providing critical care services to a critically ill or critically injured patient, even if the time spent by the physician on that date is not continuous. *Critical care* is defined as the direct delivery of medical care for a critically ill or critically injured patient by a physician(s). A critical illness or injury acutely impairs one or more vital organ systems such that there is a high probability of imminent or life-threatening deterioration in the patient's condition. For a given period of time spent, the physician must devote full attention to the patient providing critical care services and cannot provide services to any other patient during the same period. The time that can be reported as critical care is the time spent engaged in work directly related to the individual patient's care, whether that time was spent at the immediate bedside or elsewhere on the floor or unit. Time spent with the individual patient should be recorded in the patient's record. Although critical care is usually given in a critical care area, such as the coronary care unit, intensive care unit, respiratory care unit, or emergency care facility, it is not required that the patient is physically located in such an area to receive critical care services.

Code **99291** is reported once per date for the first 30 to 74 minutes of critical care even if the time spent by the physician is not continuous on that date. Critical care of less than 30 minutes in total duration on a given date should be reported with the appropriate E/M code. Code **99292** is used to report additional block(s) of time of up to 30 minutes each, beyond the first 74 minutes. When critical care services are provided in the outpatient setting, code **99291** or **99292** is reported regardless of the age of the patient.

Services included in the critical care codes are as follows:

- Interpretation of cardiac output measurements (**93561**, **93562**)
- Chest x-rays (**71010**, **71075**, **71020**)
- Pulse oximetry (**94760**, **94761**, **94762**)
- Blood gases and information data stored in computers (eg, electrocardiograms, blood pressures, hematologic data) (**99090**)
- Gastric intubation (**43752**, **91105**)
- Temporary transcutaneous pacing (**92953**)
- Ventilator management (**94656**, **94657**, **94660**, **94662**)
- Vascular access procedures (**36000**, **36410**, **36415**, **36540**, **36600**)

Any services performed that are not listed above should be reported separately.

Inpatient Pediatric and Neonatal Critical Care Services

The Inpatient Pediatric and Neonatal Critical Care Services codes (**99293–99296**) are reported for services provided by a physician directing the inpatient care of a critically ill neonate or infant. Codes **99293** and **99294** are reported per day, for a critically ill inpatient infant or young child from 29 days of postnatal age up through 24 months of age. Codes **99295** and **99296** are reported per day, for a critically ill inpatient neonate, from birth through 28 days of postnatal age. Codes **99293** and **99295** are reported for the first day of pediatric and neonatal care services; codes **99294** and **99296** are reported for subsequent inpatient pediatric and neonatal critical care services.

In addition to the procedures included in the hourly critical care codes (**99291** and **99292**), the following procedures are included in codes **99293–99296** and should not be reported separately. Any services performed that are not listed below may be reported separately. However, other procedures performed as a necessary part of the resuscitation (eg, endotracheal intubation, code **31500**), are also reported separately when performed as a part of the preadmission delivery room care. To report these procedures separately, they must be *performed as a necessary component of the resuscitation* and not simply as a convenience before admission to the neonatal intensive care unit.

Additional services included in the pediatric and neonatal critical care service codes are as follows:

- Umbilical venous catheter (**36510**)
- Umbilical arterial catheter (**36660**)
- Central (**36555**) or peripheral (**36000**) vessel catheterization
- Other arterial catheters (**36140**, **36620**)
- Oral or nasogastric tube placement (**43752**)
- Endotracheal intubation (**31500**)
- Lumbar puncture (**62270**)
- Suprapubic bladder aspiration (**51000**)
- Bladder catheterization (**53670**)
- Initiation and management of mechanical ventilation (**94656**, **94657**)
- Continuous positive airway pressure (CPAP) (**94660**)
- Surfactant administration, intravascular fluid administration (**90780**, **90781**)
- Transfusion of blood components (**36430**, **36440**)
- Vascular punctures (**36420**, **36600**)
- Bedside pulmonary function testing (**94375**)
- Monitoring or interpretation of blood gases or oxygen saturation (**94760–94762**)

Intensive (Non-Critical) Low Birth Weight Services

The Intensive (Non-Critical) Low Birth Weight Services codes (**99298** and **99299**) are reported once per day, for intensive care (noncritical) services provided to low-birth-weight (LBW) or very-low-birth-weight (VLBW) neonates or infants who no longer are considered critically ill but who require intensive observation and frequent services and interventions available only in an intensive care setting. Code **99298** describes subsequent intensive care, per day, for the evaluation and management of the recovering VLBW infant (present body weight less than 1500 grams). Code **99299** describes subsequent intensive care, per day, for the evaluation and management of the recovering LBW infant (present body weight of 1500–2500 grams). Codes **99298** and **99299** are global 24-hour codes with the same services included (bundled) under codes **99293–99296**.

Nursing Facility Services

The Nursing Facility Services codes (**99301–99316**) are reported for services provided to patients in nursing facilities (formerly called skilled nursing facilities [SNFs], intermediate care facilities [ICFs], or long-term care facilities [LTCFs]) and psychiatric residential treatment centers.

There are three subcategories of Nursing Facility Services codes: Comprehensive Nursing Facility Assessments; Subsequent Nursing Facility Care; and Nursing Facility Discharge Services. Nursing facilities have the responsibility to conduct comprehensive assessments of each resident's functional capacity by means of a resident assessment instrument (RAI). An RAI is a form composed of a uniform minimum data set (MDS) and resident assessment protocols (RAPs).

Comprehensive Nursing Facility Assessments

The Comprehensive Nursing Facility Assessments codes (**99301–99303**) help to ensure the physician's involvement whenever one of these events takes place. Three codes describe each of the three events that trigger the performance of a comprehensive assessment by the facility. If the patient is admitted to the nursing facility in the course of an encounter in another site of service, the nursing facility level of service should include the services related to the admission that were provided in the other sites of service as well as in the nursing facility setting, when performed on the same date as the admission or readmission. However, when hospital or observation discharge services performed on the same date as the nursing facility admission or readmission are reported, they may be reported separately.

Subsequent Nursing Facility Care

Subsequent Nursing Facility Care codes (**99311–99313**) are reported for the services provided to a patient whose condition or status does not require a comprehensive assessment by either the physician or the nursing facility, and/or who have not had a major permanent change of status.

Nursing Facility Discharge Services

The Nursing Facility Discharge Services codes (**99315** and **99316**) are time based and are intended to be reported for the total duration of time spent by the physician for the final nursing facility discharge of the patient, even if the time spent providing the service is not continuous. Only one code is reported: code **99315** if the total time is 30 minutes or less, or code **99316** if the total time is more than 30 minutes. Like the Hospital Discharge Services codes, the Nursing

Facility Discharge Services codes may be used to report discharge services provided to patients who die during the nursing facility stay. The attending physician would perform the final examination of the patient (pronouncing the patient dead), discussing the nursing facility stay with family members or others, and preparing discharge records.

Domiciliary, Rest Home (eg, Boarding Home), or Custodial Care Services

The Domiciliary, Rest Home (eg, Boarding Home), or Custodial Care Services category of codes (**99321–99333**) is used to report E/M services provided in a facility that provides room, board, and other personal assistance services, generally on a long-term basis. (Note that facility services do not include a medical component.)

Home Services

The Home Services codes (**99341–99350**) are used to report provision of E/M services in the patient's private residence by the physician. There are separate subcategories of codes for new patient and established patient visits. For nonphysician health care professionals providing services in the home setting, codes **99500–99602** in the Home Health Procedures/Services subsection of the Medicine section should be reported.

Prolonged Services

The Prolonged Services codes (**99354–99360**) are used to report the provision of prolonged services by a physician that are beyond the usual services provided in either an inpatient or outpatient setting. There are three separate subcategories of codes used to distinguish prolonged services involving direct (face-to-face) patient contact (**99354–99357**), prolonged physician services without direct (face-to-face) patient contact (**99358** and **99359**), and physician standby services (**99360**).

Prolonged Physician Services With Direct (Face-to-Face) Patient Contact

The Prolonged Physician Services With Direct (Face-to-Face) Patient Contact codes (**99354–99357**) are used when a physician provides prolonged service involving direct (face-to-face) patient contact that is beyond the usual service (ie, beyond the typical time) in either the inpatient or outpatient setting. The term *face-to-face* refers only to patient face-to-face contact. These are time-based codes and reported for the total duration of face-to-face time spent by a physician providing prolonged services on a given date. It is not necessary for the time spent by the physician providing the prolonged service to be continuous. These codes are all add-on codes and are reported separately, in addition to the appropriate code for the E/M service provided.

Codes **99354** and **99355** are reported for the office or other outpatient setting. Codes **99356** and **99357** are reported for the inpatient setting.

Codes **99354** and **99356** are used to report the first hour of prolonged service. These codes may also be used to report a total duration of prolonged service of 30 to 60 minutes on a given date. Prolonged service of less than 30 minutes in total duration on a given date is not reported separately. Less than 30 minutes of prolonged service is included in the E/M code reported for that date. Codes **99355** and **99357** are used to report each additional 30 minutes beyond the first hour of prolonged services. These codes may also be used to report the final 15 to 30 minutes of prolonged service on a given date.

Prolonged service of less than 15 minutes beyond the first hour or less than 15 minutes beyond the final 30 minutes is not separately reported.

Prolonged Physician Services Without Direct (Face-To-Face) Patient Contact

The Prolonged Physician Services Without Direct (Face-To-Face) Patient Contact codes (**99358** and **99359**) are used to report prolonged services without direct (face-to-face) patient contact in either the inpatient or outpatient setting. The total duration of time spent providing these services on a given date is reported, even if the time spent by the physician on that date is not continuous. Prolonged services of less than 30 minutes in total duration on a given date are not reported. These codes are considered add-on codes and are reported separately, in addition to the code(s) for other physician services and/or inpatient or outpatient E/M service. Code **99358** is intended to be reported separately in addition to code(s) for other physician service(s) and/or an inpatient or outpatient E/M service. Code **99358** must first be reported to report code **99359**.

Code **99358** is used to report the first hour of prolonged service on a given date, regardless of the place of service. This code may also be used to report a total duration of prolonged service of 30 to 60 minutes on a given date. It should be reported only once per patient, per date, even if the time spent by the physician is not continuous on that date.

Code **99359** is used to report each additional 30 minutes beyond the first hour of prolonged physician services, again regardless of the place of service. It may also be used to report the final 15 to 30 minutes of prolonged service on a given date. Prolonged service of less than 15 minutes beyond the first hour or less than 15 minutes beyond the final 30 minutes is not reported separately.

Physician Standby Services

The Physician Standby Services code (**99360**) is used to report physician standby services requiring prolonged physician attendance without direct (face-to-face) patient contact. Physician standby services are provided at the request of another physician. This code is used to report a total duration of 30 minutes of physician standby service on a given date. Standby services of less than 30 minutes on a given date are not reported separately. If an additional full 30 minutes of a standby service is provided, it is appropriate to report code **99360** for each full 30 minutes of standby service.

To report code **99360**, the physician must be available to provide care to the patient, but may not actually provide any care. The physician providing the standby services cannot provide care or services to other patients during the period of standby.

This code is not reported by the standby physician if the period of standby ends with his or her performance of a procedure subject to a "surgical package." It is also not appropriate to report this code for time spent proctoring another physician.

Case Management Services

Physician *case management* is a process in which a physician is responsible for the direct care of a patient, coordinating and controlling access to health care services needed by the patient, and initiating and/or supervising other health care services needed by the patient. The Case Management Services codes include two subcategories: Team Conferences and Telephone Calls.

Team Conferences

The Team Conferences codes (**99361** and **99362**) are time-based codes used to report a medical conference by a physician with an interdisciplinary team of health care professionals or representatives of community agencies to coordinate activities of patient care. The patient is not present during the conference. Code **99361** is reported for a medical conference of approximately 30 minutes in duration. Code **99362** is reported for a medical conference of approximately 60 minutes in duration.

Telephone Calls

The Telephone Calls codes (**99371–99373**) are used for reporting telephone calls by a physician. Each code has a lengthy descriptor that includes examples of the type of service that may be provided when the code is reported. Code **99371** is used to report a phone call that is simple or brief, **99372** is used to report an intermediate phone call, and code **99373** describes a phone call that is complex or lengthy. When these codes are reported, the phone call *must* be made by the *physician*, and not by the nurse or other physician office personnel.

Care Plan Oversight Services

Care Plan Oversight Services codes (**99374–99380**) are reported for physician supervision of patients under the care of a home health agency, a hospice, or a nursing facility.

All of the codes are time based and used to report the complexity and approximate physician time of the care plan oversight services provided within a 30-day period (within a calendar month) of time.

Preventive Medicine Services

The Preventive Medicine Services codes (**99381–99429**) include initial preventive medicine E/M services for new patient visits and periodic preventive medicine reevaluation and management services for established patient visits. The codes for initial and periodic preventive medicine E/M services are categorized by patient age. There are also codes for preventive medicine counseling for individuals and groups.

The preventive medicine E/M codes for new and established patients include a comprehensive history and a comprehensive examination. The comprehensive nature of the Preventive Medicine Services codes reflects an age- and gender-appropriate history/examination and is not synonymous with the comprehensive examination required in E/M codes **99201–99350**.

The comprehensive history obtained as part of the preventive medicine E/M service is not problem-oriented and does not involve a chief complaint or present illness. It does, however, include a comprehensive system review and comprehensive or interval past, family, and social history, as well as a comprehensive assessment/history of pertinent risk factors. The comprehensive examination performed as part of the preventive medicine E/M service is multisystem, but the extent of the examination is based on the age of the patient and the risk factors identified.

If an abnormality is encountered or a preexisting problem is addressed in the process of performing the preventive medicine E/M service, and the problem is significant enough to require additional work for the physician to perform the key components of a problem-oriented E/M service, then the appropriate Office or Other Outpatient Service code (**99201–99215**) should be reported in addition to the appropriate code for the preventive E/M service. Modifier 25 should be appended to the office/outpatient code reported. Appending modifier 25 indicates that a significant, separately identifiable E/M service (above and beyond the preventive medicine E/M service) was provided by the same physician on the same day as the preventive medicine service. If a physician encounters an insignificant or trivial problem or abnormality in the process of performing the preventive medicine E/M service that does not require additional work and the performance of the key components of a problem-oriented service, then it would not be appropriate to report the problem-oriented service in addition to the preventive services.

The codes for new and established patient preventive medicine E/M services *include* counseling, anticipatory guidance, and risk factor reduction interventions that are provided at the time of the initial or periodic preventive medicine service. Counseling and/or risk factor reduction interventions provided at a *separate encounter* for the purpose of promoting health and preventing illness or injury are reported with codes **99401–99412**. Immunizations and ancillary studies involving laboratory, radiology, other procedures, or screening tests identified with a specific CPT code are reported separately.

Newborn Care

Newborn Care codes (**99431–99440**) are used to report E/M services provided to normal (well) newborns in several different settings. If a critical condition is observed in the newborn during the E/M service (**99431–99435**) and the newborn subsequently receives critical care services in or outside of a neonatal critical care unit, codes **99295** and **99296** would also be reported as defined in the Critical Care subsection of this chapter. Physician Standby Services (**99360**), Attendance at Delivery and Initial Stabilization of Newborn (**99436**), and Newborn Resuscitation (**99440**) may be used on the same day as the initial (neonatal intensive care unit admission) critical care service (**99295**). If the newborn is transferred to another facility to receive critical care services, and the physician accompanies the newborn and manages the care of the patient during the transport, codes **99289** and **99290** should be reported. The pediatric transport codes **99289** and **99290** may be reported in addition to the neonatal or pediatric initial (admission) critical care codes (**99293–99296**).

Chapter 1

Evaluation and Management Services Exercises

EXERCISE 1

Consultation vs Initial Office Visit

A young man went to his primary care physician with a chief complaint of low back pain with some discomfort radiating into his right leg. He was diagnosed with a lumbosacral strain and "sciatica" and treated with nonsteroidal anti-inflammatory medication and muscle relaxants. The symptoms did not improve, and he returned to his primary care physician with worsening back pain and leg pain as well as numbness, tingling, and weakness. The primary care physician requested that the patient see a physiatrist for further evaluation, advice, and/or opinion on the proper course of treatment. The following day, he was seen by the physiatrist, who performed a thorough history and physical examination at the request of the primary care physician. A diagnosis of lumbosacral disk herniation with radiculopathy was made. The physiatrist recommended a trial of oral steroids and prescribed a detailed physical therapy program. If there was insufficient clinical improvement within one week or any worsening of the patient's neurologic symptoms, the physiatrist would recommend magnetic resonance imaging of the lumbosacral spine. The physiatrist sent a summary of the findings and recommendations to the primary care physician.

Should a consultation or an initial office visit (referral) be reported?

EXERCISE 2

Neonatal and Pediatric Critical Care

A baby girl aged one month two days was seen in the emergency department because of difficulty in breathing. The emergency department physician administered one hour of critical care services to the baby girl. The pediatrician subsequently (same date) admitted the patient to the pediatric intensive care unit.

Which code(s) should the emergency department physician and pediatrician report for their critical care services?

A. **99291** *Critical care, evaluation and management of the critically ill or critically injured patient; first 30-74 minutes* [by the emergency department physician]
and
99293 *Initial inpatient pediatric critical care, 29 days up through 24 months of age, per day, for the evaluation and management of a critically ill infant or young child* [by the pediatrician]

CODING TIP

If, during the visit, the mother had raised a concern or the physician had discovered an abnormality that the physician proceeded to address during the visit, an appropriate office/outpatient visit code (**99201–99215**) should also be reported. If the problem was significant enough to require additional work to perform the key components of a problem-oriented E/M service, modifier 25 should be added to the problem-oriented E/M code.

B. **99293** *Initial inpatient pediatric critical care, 29 days up through 24 months of age, per day, for the evaluation and management of a critically ill infant or young child* [reported twice, once by the emergency department physician and once by the pediatrician]

C. **99291** *Critical care, evaluation and management of the critically ill or critically injured patient; first 30–74 minutes* [by the emergency department physician]

and

99295 *Initial inpatient neonatal critical care, per day, for the evaluation and management of a critically ill neonate, 29 days of age or less* [by the pediatrician]

EXERCISE 3

Preventive Medicine

An 18-month-old boy was brought to his regular physician's office for his 18-month checkup. According to his mother, he was doing fine. He was eating table food and slept through the night. Progress note indicates the following:

Subjective: Patient is here for his 18-month checkup. His mother reports no problems and no recent illnesses. He is eating table food, sleeps through the night, and goes to a play group twice a week. He is walking and running without difficulty and does not tire easily. He plays appropriately with others his age.

Objective: Weight, 22 lb; length, 31 in; temperature, 98.6°F
HEENTN: Nl, ears Nl, pharynx Nl
Lungs: clear
Heart: heart tones normal, no extra sounds, no thrill
Abdomen: no masses; no organomegaly; no tenderness
Genitourinary: both testicles descended
Extremities: normal, legs straight
Central Nervous System: normal for age
Skin: no lesions
Denver Developmental Screening Test: passes all

Assessment: Normal 18-month check

Plan: DTaP – 4. Anticipatory guidance and accident prevention discussed with mother.

How is this procedure reported?

EXERCISE 4

Preventive Medicine

A 22-year-old, male, established patient came to the physician's office seeking information about HIV. He did not want an examination but said he wanted to learn all he could from "an expert" rather than from his friends. The physician's progress note stated the following:

Patient came in asking to learn about HIV. He said he is not sure if what he hears on the street is true and has come here to learn the facts. He said he is not sexually active but that he may become sexually active in the near future. He said that he is heterosexual. HIV was discussed with the patient in terms of what it is, how it affects the immune system, how it is spread, how to decrease the chance of becoming infected, and safer sex. Total length of time spent counseling the patient was 30 minutes.

How is this procedure reported?

EXERCISE 5

Emergency Department

A 20-year-old male was dropped off in front of the hospital emergency department (ED) with a knife hilt sticking out of his mid-left anterior chest. The patient was not fully conscious. No one accompanied him. The patient was transported into the ED and the attending ED physician began the evaluation. Physical examination was less than comprehensive, but it was noted that whenever there was a peripheral pulse, the knife handle quivered. The attending ED physician initiated trauma team mobilization and ordered necessary diagnostics and fluid/blood replacement products. A partial history was obtained and documented by the attending ED physician. Care of the patient proceeded under the attending ED physician's management. Twenty minutes after the patient was brought into the ED, the on-call trauma surgeon arrived in the ED, and the attending ED physician transferred care of the patient to the surgeon. The patient's need for a high-level E/M service and inability to provide a comprehensive history, as well as the unsuitability of an initial comprehensive examination, was evident in the medical record.

How is this procedure reported?

EXERCISE 6

Emergency Department/Critical Care

A 61-year-old patient walked into the ED complaining of "pressure on my chest." The attending ED physician evaluated the patient, including a full interpretation of a 12-lead electrocardiogram (ECG). Among the findings of the ECG interpretation were signs of acute cardiac damage, but no arrhythmia. The attending ED physician provided appropriate initial management and contacted the attending admitting physician, who happened to be in the hospital. Arrangements were made to admit the patient to the cardiac care unit. When the attending admitting physician came to the ED, the attending ED physician transferred care of the patient to her. Unfortunately, there were no beds immediately available in the cardiac care unit, and so the patient had to be held in the ED. After evaluating the patient, the admitting physician left the ED.

Three hours later, the patient was still in the ED and, during a period of 80 minutes, experienced acute difficulty breathing, increased chest pain, arrhythmias (as noted on a cardiac monitor), and a cardiopulmonary arrest. During this 80-minute period, the attending ED physician provided critical care services for the patient, provided a full interpretation of a new 12-lead ECG at the beginning of the 80 minutes, performed endotracheal intubation, directed hospital personnel's efforts to restore the patient's breathing and circulation for 20 minutes, and interpreted one lead of a third ECG printout. The resuscitation attempt was unsuccessful. The physician noted a total critical care service provision time of 44 minutes, exclusive of other separately reportable services.

What code(s) should the ED physician report?

EXERCISE 7

Prolonged Services

A 55-year-old male was referred to a neurologist because of leg weakness and sensory loss that had begun after surgery two years earlier. On the basis of his evaluation, the neurologist suspected a thoracic myelopathy. He was most concerned about a spinal cord infarct or space-occupying lesion in the thoracic cord. The patient arrived at the appointment without medical records from the surgery and the many physicians he had seen in the intervening two years. The neurologist suggested that the patient make another appointment, requesting that he bring copies of the medical records and imaging studies. The patient returned in one month, toting 2 inches of paper records and a large number of x-ray jackets containing plain x-rays, magnetic resonance imaging scans, computed tomography scans, and a myelogram. Because the patient complained of greater leg weakness and stiffness, the neurologist reexamined the patient, performing a *detailed* history and physical examination. He spent 75 minutes face-to-face with the patient, reviewing the medical records and imaging studies, clarifying the patient's problem with further questioning, and explaining the diagnostic and treatment options to the patient. He decided to perform a lumbar puncture on the patient the next day and prescribed for the patient baclofen for spasticity and carbamazepine for neuropathic pain.

How is the second office visit coded?

EXERCISE 8

Critical Care Services

A 72-year-old female was seen in the emergency department of a city hospital within half an hour of a sudden onset of left hemiplegia and atrial fibrillation. The hospital's neurology acute stroke service was paged and the neurologist assumed responsibility for management of the patient. It was necessary for the neurologist to administer critical care services. When the neurologist first evaluated the patient and performed the National Institutes of Health stroke scale in the emergency department, her blood pressure was 220/110 mm Hg. A computed tomography scan was performed and was normal in the judgment of the neurologist. The patient's blood pressure decreased to 180/110 mm Hg within one and one-half hours after the onset of her stroke. The neurologist reevaluated the patient and ordered administration of a thrombolytic agent in the emergency department, with an initial 10% bolus and the remainder administered during a one-hour period through an intravenous catheter infusion. The neurologist admitted the patient to the intensive care unit (ICU). When the infusion was complete and the neurologist had finished performing subsequent evaluations, the neurologist had spent approximately two and one-half hours managing and performing critical care services for the patient in the emergency department and the ICU. The ICU nursing staff continued to manage the patient's blood pressure and monitor her vital signs.

What E/M services code(s) should the neurologist report?

CHAPTER 2

Anesthesia

OBJECTIVES

This chapter will assist in accomplishing the following objectives:

- Understand the anesthesia guidelines for coding anesthesia services and any additional procedures/services provided
- Understand basic anesthesia administration services
- Understand which services are included when the Current Procedural Terminology (CPT®) codes for anesthesia are reported

Introduction to Anesthesia

Coding for the administration of anesthesia and any additional procedures or services may appear to be straightforward; however, widely varying payer reporting requirements can add complexity to coding for both categories of services. An understanding of the anesthesia guidelines is the first step in learning how to properly code for anesthesia services and any additional procedures or services provided.

Basic anesthesia administration services are those services provided by, or under the responsible supervision of, a physician and include the following:

- Routine preoperative and postoperative visits to evaluate the patient for the planned anesthesia and monitor the patient's postsurgery recovery from anesthesia
- Administration of fluids and/or blood during the period of anesthesia care
- Interpretation of noninvasive monitoring such as electrocardiography (ECG), body temperature, blood pressure, oximetry (blood oxygen concentration), capnography (blood carbon dioxide concentration), and mass spectrometry

Unusual invasive forms of monitoring (such as intra-arterial, central venous, and pulmonary artery catheters, and transesophageal echocardiography) are not included in basic anesthesia administration services. When these procedures are performed, they should be reported separately according to standard CPT coding guidelines applicable to the given code and the respective section in the CPT codebook in which they are listed.

Anesthesia administration services may be reported by using the appropriate code in the Anesthesia section of the CPT codebook (codes **00100-01999**), the appropriate anesthesia modifier, and qualifying circumstances codes, as appropriate. However, some payers do not accept CPT Anesthesia codes, and instead require the use of code(s) from the Surgery section of the CPT codebook for reporting anesthesia services. This practice may cause problems because the anesthesia services often cannot be distinguished from any additional procedures or services provided by the anesthesiologist. It is critical to develop an understanding of CPT coding guidelines and payer-specific guidelines for reporting anesthesia services. A clear distinction must be made between services provided when coding is done.

Generally, a single code is reported for anesthesia administration whether the operating physician performs one or multiple procedures. When multiple procedures are performed during a single anesthetic administration, only the anesthesia procedure code for the most complex service and the total time for all procedures are reported. Anesthesia add-on codes are an exception. Codes **01953**, **01968**, and **01969** describe anesthesia add-on procedures, which are reported in addition to the primary anesthesia code.

Code Descriptors Including Phrases "With Anesthesia" or "Requiring Anesthesia"

It should be noted that there are certain CPT code descriptors in the CPT codebook that include the phrases, *with anesthesia* or *requiring anesthesia*. These phrases indicate that the work involved in performing that procedure requires anesthesia, whether it is general anesthesia, regional anesthesia, or monitored anesthesia care. The appropriate anesthesia code is separately reported. Conscious sedation is not an anesthesia service.

Monitored Anesthesia Care

Monitored anesthesia care (MAC) is a specific anesthesia service for a diagnostic or therapeutic procedure. Indications for MAC include the nature of the procedure, the patient's clinical condition, and/or the potential need to convert to a general or regional anesthetic.

Monitored anesthesia care includes all aspects of anesthesia care: a preprocedure visit, intraprocedure care, and postprocedure anesthesia management. During MAC, the anesthesiologist provides or medically directs a number of specific services, including but not limited to:

- Diagnosis and treatment of clinical problems that occur during the procedure
- Support of vital functions
- Administration of sedatives, analgesics, hypnotics, anesthetic agents, or other medications as necessary for patient safety
- Psychological support and physical comfort
- Provision of other medical services as needed to complete the procedure safely

Monitored anesthesia care may include varying levels of sedation, analgesia, and anxiolysis as necessary. The provider of MAC must be prepared and qualified to convert to general anesthesia when necessary. If the patient loses consciousness and the ability to respond purposefully, the anesthesia care is a general anesthetic, regardless of whether airway instrumentation is required.

Monitored anesthesia care is a physician service provided to an individual patient. It should be subject to the same level of reimbursement as general or regional anesthesia. Accordingly, the American Society of Anesthesiologists (ASA) Relative Value Guide provides for the use of proper basic procedural units, time units, and modifier units as the basis for determining reimbursement.

Chapter 2

Anesthesia Exercises

EXERCISE 1

A patient undergoing a thoracotomy received a continuous epidural injection of a local anesthetic and/or narcotic for relief of postoperative pain in addition to a general anesthetic, which was administered in part through an endotracheal tube.

What is the appropriate anesthesia code and surgical code to report?

EXERCISE 2

History: The patient was a young adult athlete who had sustained an injury to the knee and had a painful and unstable knee that precluded athletic participation. A magnetic resonance imaging examination showed a torn anterior cruciate ligament, and an arthroscopically assisted surgical repair of the torn anterior cruciate ligament was scheduled.

Preanesthesia: The patient was evaluated in the outpatient preanesthesia clinic. The patient's medical history was reviewed and a physical examination was performed with special emphasis on the airway and respiratory and cardiovascular systems. Various options of anesthetic management were discussed with the patient, including general anesthetic with peripheral nerve block for postoperative pain control or regional anesthesia to include spinal, epidural, and peripheral nerve block. The patient requested general anesthesia with peripheral nerve block for postoperative pain control. In the preanesthesia area, the patient was reexamined and the choice of anesthetic was reaffirmed. Oxygen saturation was monitored, intravenous access was established, and sedation was administered. A femoral nerve block was performed with the use of a nerve stimulator to ensure appropriate needle placement. After completion of the femoral nerve block, the patient was taken to the operating room.

Intra-anesthesia: General anesthesia was induced after monitors were applied and baseline vital functions were assessed. An inhalation anesthetic was used with a laryngeal mask airway. The procedure, which included an open harvest of the patellar tendon graft and the arthroscopic preparation of the joint and placement of the graft, proceeded without problem. Vital signs were monitored continuously during the procedure. Inhalation and intravenous anesthetic agents were titrated as needed. At the end of the procedure, and after the placement of a brace on the operated-on knee, the patient was awakened and the laryngeal mask airway removed. The patient was taken to the postanesthesia care unit.

Postanesthesia: The anesthesiologist wrote orders for postoperative pain relief and therapy for nausea. Upon awakening, the patient was comfortable, with anesthesia over the distribution of the femoral nerve block. Before discharge from the outpatient recovery area, the patient was evaluated for postanesthetic problems and was given the opportunity to ask questions about the anesthetic.

What is the appropriate anesthesia code and surgical code to report?

EXERCISE 3

Primary Cesarean Delivery With Epidural Anesthesia for Labor for Planned Vaginal Delivery

History: A 30-year-old primiparous female was seen in labor; estimated fetal age was 41 weeks.

Preanesthesia: The patient's medical history was unremarkable and she had no previous anesthetic experience. After maternal and fetal assessment, intravenous access was established. Initial labor pain was treated with intravenous butorphanol. The anesthesiologist was consulted because of increased discomfort and lack of relief with butorphanol. The anesthesiologist reviewed the patient's chart and examined the patient with particular attention to the airway, heart, lungs, and spine. Alternatives and relative risks of anesthesia management were discussed with the patient. The anesthesiologist recommended the placement of a lumbar epidural through which a continuous infusion of local anesthetic and narcotic could be infused to provide analgesia for labor and anticipated vaginal delivery.

Intra-anesthesia: The patient was appropriately hydrated with intravenous fluids. She was then placed in the sitting position and the appropriate landmarks were identified. After preparation of the necessary equipment, the patient's back was sterilely prepped and the epidural catheter was placed. Blood pressure, fetal heart rate, and dermatone level of analgesia were regularly checked. A time-based anesthesia record was developed to record expected and unexpected changes in blood pressure and fetal heart rates. The progress of labor was monitored. The patient was visited regularly by the anesthesiologist and the infusion was adjusted to meet the patient's analgesic needs. After seven hours of epidural infusion, the patient's cervix was noted to be completely dilated, though the fetal vertex remained high. The labor nurse reported that there was a moderate amount of meconium staining. Maternal efforts to push the fetus out were started. After three hours of maternal efforts at pushing, the fetal heart tones were noted to have increased to 190 beats per minute with a loss of variability. Cesarean delivery was indicated. The anesthesiologist again reviewed the notes of the labor nurse and discussed the alternatives of anesthesia for the cesarean delivery with the patient. Epidural anesthesia, using the already functioning catheter, was recommended. The surgical suite was prepared to ensure proper function of the anesthesia machine, the adequacy of the oxygen supply, the presence of suction equipment, and the preparation of anesthesia drugs, especially those to induce general anesthesia should it be necessary. The patient was transferred to the operating suite, with care taken to protect against dislodgment of the epidural catheter. Blood pressure, electrocardiogram, and pulse oximetry monitors were applied. Oxygen was provided by mask. Fetal heart tones were checked. Two percent lidocaine was injected through the epidural catheter to achieve a level of surgical anesthesia. Intravenous fluids were administered in amounts to meet surgical blood loss and maintenance requirements. Lower blood pressure was anticipated because of the sympathetic blockade as a part of the epidural anesthesia. After cessation of surgery, preservative-free morphine or fentanyl was injected through the epidural catheter to enhance postoperative analgesia. The patient was transported to the postanesthesia care unit. Vital signs, dermatome level of anesthesia, oxygen saturation, and adequacy of ventilation were determined. Supplemental analgesia was provided with intravenous narcotics. Fluids and vasopressors were administered as necessary to maintain adequate blood pressure and urine output. After the level of epidural anesthesia had subsided, vital signs stabilized, and adequate analgesia was achieved, the patient was discharged to the postpartum unit.

Postanesthesia: Management of epidural narcotics and supplemental analgesia for 24 hours was ordered. Additional care was provided as indicated or requested by the obstetrician.

What is the appropriate anesthesia code and surgical code to report?

EXERCISE 4

History: The patient was involved in a motor vehicle accident and sustained an acetabular wall dislocation fracture. He had multiple system involvement. His unstable condition warranted the placement of an arterial catheter (reported separately) as well as a central venous line (reported separately) by the anesthesiologist to obtain more than the usual level of monitoring and to facilitate the rapid administration of large volumes of blood and/or other fluids and cardiovascular support.

Preanesthesia: The anesthesiologist evaluated the patient in the intensive care unit. The patient's recent clinical course and vital signs were reviewed. The anesthesiologist reviewed the medical record and the anesthetic record and progress notes from the previous evening. A full report was obtained from the nurse. Neither neurosurgery nor orthopedic surgery was able to adequately determine cervical spine stability. In addition, the recent notes by the trauma surgeon as well as the consulting orthopedic, plastic, and general surgeons were reviewed. Current laboratory data and imaging studies were reviewed. A directed physical examination was performed with special attention to pulmonary, cardiac, and mental status. Plans, risks, and expectations were reviewed with the patient and family, and all questions were answered as consent was obtained for the planned anesthetic care.

Intra-anesthesia: Venous access sites were examined and a new 14-gauge peripheral intravenous line was placed. A radial artery was cannulated (separately reported). In addition, a central venous pressure monitor (separately reported) was placed into the jugular or subclavian veins to assess volume status during the periods of rapid blood loss. At this time, topicalization for the patient's airway had begun by both local anesthetic spray and a translaryngeal injection. The patient was transferred to the operating room, continuously monitored by the anesthesiologist and with oxygen being continued by face mask. Additional intravenous analgesics were administered before the patient was carefully moved to the operating table. Electrocardiogram, noninvasive blood pressure, and pulse oximetry monitoring were reestablished. Before general anesthesia was induced, further topical anesthesia and intravenous sedation were provided and gas analysis, including end-tidal CO_2 monitoring, was initiated. An endotracheal tube was placed, and after correct positioning was confirmed with auscultation and end-tidal CO_2 analysis, the endotracheal tube was secured and mechanical ventilation commenced. Mild hypotension after induction was corrected pharmacologically with agents that had been prepared in advance. Inhalational anesthetics were titrated to maintain anesthesia. A high-flow fluid warmer with intravenous fluids was prepared and attached to the recently placed 14-gauge intravenous line. A forced-air warming blanket was placed and an esophageal stethoscope/temperature probe was inserted orally to attempt to maintain normothermia. Careful attention was given to positioning and padding, as the potential existed for a prolonged surgery. Inhalational anesthetics and intravenous narcotics were carefully titrated to maintain anesthesia and hemodynamic stability. Neuromuscular blockade was regularly monitored by means of peripheral nerve stimulation, and additional paralytic agents were administered to maintain adequate surgical relaxation. Intravenous fluids were administered at a rapid rate to replace substantial insensible losses and surgical blood loss. Urinary output and temperature were monitored. Throughout the duration of the procedure, surgical blood loss was assessed and treated and stable hemodynamics were maintained. This assessment and treatment was generally quite complex. as there was massive bleeding. Retroperitoneal hematoma was present. Shock was a concern. Arterial blood gases were intermittently analyzed and the central venous pressure was continually evaluated, and any abnormalities were addressed. As the surgical procedure neared completion, adequacy of neuromuscular function was determined, inhalational anesthetics were gradually reduced, and weaning the patient from mechanical ventilation was attempted. Depending on the various intraoperative conditions, the patient may begin to breathe spontaneously and morphine is titrated intravenously to provide analgesia yet allow for planned extubation at the conclusion of the procedure. The patient's level of consciousness, ventilatory efforts, capnogram, and oximetry are assessed to determine the adequacy of spontaneous respiration. If these parameters appear satisfactory, the patient is extubated and mask oxygen administered. Otherwise the patient will remain on full ventilatory support and taken directly to the intensive care unit. The patient is then transported to the postanesthesia care unit with continuous oxygen by mask or transported directly to the intensive care unit on full ventilatory support.

Postanesthesia: In the postanesthesia care unit, a patient history and synopsis of intraoperative events, including fluids administered, blood loss, urinary output, drugs administered, and vital sign trends, was provided to the nursing staff. The anesthesiologist continued to participate in the management of postoperative analgesia, fluid balance, and respiratory care while the patient was cared for in the postanesthesia care unit. When the patient was stable, the anesthesiologist discharged him from the postanesthesia care unit. The patient was seen again the next day to evaluate his recovery from anesthesia and determine whether any anesthesia-related complications occurred.

What is the appropriate anesthesia code and surgical code to report?

CHAPTER 3

Surgery

OBJECTIVES

This chapter will assist in accomplishing the following objectives:

- Understand the Current Procedural Terminology (CPT®) Surgical Package definition
- Become familiar with the Surgery subsections and understand the guidelines that are unique to reporting codes from the subsections
- Identify when more than one code is necessary to accurately report a procedure

Introduction to Surgery

The Surgery section is the largest section of the CPT codebook. When a code is chosen from the Surgery section, it is important to be aware of some basic guidelines. Because CPT nomenclature is not a strict classification system, there may be some procedures that appear in sections other than those where they ordinarily might be classified. The name of the procedure or service that most accurately identifies the service performed should be selected.

When procedures are evaluated for reporting, reimbursement, or other purposes, it is essential that each procedure be considered on its own merits, not simply on the basis of the location or placement of the code in the CPT codebook. Also, the listing of a service or procedure and its code number in a particular subsection of the Surgery section does not restrict its use to a specific specialty group. Any procedure or service in *any* section of the CPT codebook, or any subsection of service in the Surgery section, may be used to report the services and procedures performed by any qualified physician. Guidelines that define items that are necessary to appropriately interpret and report the procedures and services within each subsection are presented at the beginning of the Surgery section and within the subsections of the CPT codebook.

CPT Surgical Package Definition

The definition of the CPT Surgical Package can be found in the Surgery guidelines in the CPT codebook and is restated here, as follows:

> The services provided by the physician to any patient by their very nature are variable. The CPT codes that represent a readily identifiable surgical procedure thereby include, on a procedure-by-procedure basis, a variety of services. In defining the specific services "included" in a given CPT surgical code, the following services are always included in addition to the operation per se:
> - local infiltration, metacarpal/metatarsal/digital block or topical anesthesia;
> - subsequent to the decision for surgery, one related E/M encounter on the date immediately prior to or on the date of procedure (including history and physical);
> - immediate postoperative care, including dictating operative notes, talking with the family and other physicians;
> - writing orders;
> - evaluating the patient in the postanesthesia recovery area;
> - typical postoperative follow-up care.

This concept is referred to as a *package* for surgical procedures. This definition indicates that when a surgical procedure is reported with a CPT code, the items listed in that guideline are included, if they were performed, and are not reported separately.

Examples of some of these variables include:

- The type of procedure performed
- The place where the surgery occurred

- The time (during hospitalization) the surgery was performed
- The insurance contract of each individual patient

Because it is not possible to address all of these variables in a code descriptor, only the preoperative Evaluation and Management (E/M) service related to the procedure performed on the date immediately before the date of the procedure (including the history and physical) is stated as inclusive of the CPT Surgical Package definition.

Also, a specific number of postoperative days is not indicated in the CPT Surgical Package definition. CPT guidelines provide specific instructions regarding follow-up care for diagnostic procedures (eg, endoscopy, arthroscopy, injection procedures for radiography) and follow-up care for therapeutic surgical procedures. However, these guidelines do not designate a set number of days in which this follow-up care may take place. Unfortunately, there is no one standard definition of a global surgical package that is universally accepted. Services that are included in a global surgical package may differ for each third-party payer. It is important to be familiar with the reporting and reimbursement policies of the various insurance companies regarding the global surgical package.

Follow-up Care for Diagnostic and Therapeutic Surgical Procedures

CPT guidelines separately address follow-up care for diagnostic procedures and follow-up care for therapeutic surgical procedures. While a specific number of days is not described in the CPT guidelines pertaining to follow-up care, most insurance companies recognize a set number of days in which no separate payment will generally be made for services provided by the surgeon.

Follow-up care for diagnostic procedures includes only that care related to recovery from the diagnostic procedure itself. Care of the condition for which the diagnostic procedure was performed or of other coexisting conditions is not included and may be reported separately. Some examples of diagnostic procedures include endoscopy, arthroscopy, and injection procedures for radiography.

Follow-up care for therapeutic surgical procedures includes only care that is usually a part of the surgical service. Complications, exacerbations, recurrence, and the presence of other diseases or injuries requiring additional services should be separately reported.

CPT code **99024**, located in the Medicine section of the CPT codebook, is available for reporting a postoperative follow-up visit for documentation purposes only. This code is useful to the reporting physician for tracking the number of postoperative visits provided that are included in the package for the procedure performed.

Add-on Codes

Most of the procedures listed in the CPT nomenclature can be reported by themselves as stand-alone codes because they represent the total procedure that was performed; however, under certain circumstances, it may be necessary to report two or more codes to completely describe the procedures performed. Some of the codes listed in the CPT code set describe procedures or services that must never be reported as stand-alone codes. These codes are referred to as *add-on codes*. Add-on codes describe procedures or services that are always performed in addition to the primary procedure or service. They describe additional intraservice work associated with the primary procedure or service. These additional or supplemental procedures are designated as add-on codes with a ✚ symbol and are listed in Appendix D of the CPT codebook. Add-on codes can also be readily identified by specific language in the code descriptor, which includes phrases such as "each additional" or "(List separately in addition to primary procedure)." The multiple procedure modifier (51) is not appended to an add-on code, as these codes are exempt from the multiple procedure concept.

EXAMPLE

The following is an example of an add-on code.

Additional Lesion(s)

11100 Biopsy of skin, subcutaneous tissue and/or mucous membrane (including simple closure), unless otherwise listed; single lesion

✚11101 each separate/additional lesion (List separately in addition to code for primary procedure)

(Use **11101** in conjunction with code **11100**)

Code **11100** is the primary procedure and code **11101** is the add-on code. Code **11101** would never be reported without first reporting code **11100**. As the code descriptor indicates, code **11101** is reported for each separate/additional lesion. The parenthetical note following code **11101** instructs the user regarding the code that is considered the primary procedure for that particular add-on code. If biopsy is performed on three separate lesions of the skin, subcutaneous tissue, and/or mucous membrane, then code **11100** would be reported for the first lesion and code **11101** would be reported twice, once for the second lesion biopsied, and again for the third lesion biopsied.

Separate Procedure

The separate procedure concept is an important guideline in the CPT codebook to understand. Some of the codes listed in the CPT nomenclature have been identified by inclusion of the term, *separate procedure*, in the code descriptor. The separate procedure designation indicates that a certain procedure or service may be:

- Considered an integral component of another procedure or service
- Performed independently
- Unrelated
- Distinct from other procedure(s) or service(s) provided at that time

Codes designated as separate procedures may not be additionally reported when the procedure or service is performed as an integral component of another procedure or service.

EXAMPLE

The following is an example of an integral component.

58720 Salpingo-oophorectomy, complete or partial, unilateral or bilateral (separate procedure)

58150 Total abdominal hysterectomy (corpus and cervix), with or without removal of tube(s), with or without removal of ovary(s)

When a total abdominal hysterectomy with removal of the tube(s) and ovary(s) is reported, it would not be appropriate to separately report code **58720** in conjunction with code **58150**. The procedure described by code **58720** is considered an integral component of the procedures described by code **58150**.

However, codes designated as separate procedures should be additionally reported when performed independently, unrelated, or distinct from other procedure(s) or service(s) provided.

EXAMPLE

The following is an example of a procedure performed independently.

58720 Salpingo-oophorectomy, complete or partial, unilateral or bilateral (separate procedure)

If removal of the fallopian tubes and ovaries is the only procedure performed, then it would be appropriate to report code **58720** to describe the procedure performed.

EXAMPLE

The following is an example of unrelated procedures.

56605 Biopsy of vulva or perineum (separate procedure); one lesion

49505 Repair initial inguinal hernia, age 5 years or over; reducible

Biopsy of the vulva or perineum is a procedure that is unrelated to repair of an inguinal hernia. In this example, if the same physician performed both of these procedures, then it would be appropriate to report both codes to fully describe the procedures performed. Modifier 59 (distinct procedural service) would be appended to code **49505** to indicate that the procedure was performed independently and **56605** to indicate that the procedure was unrelated to the repair of the inguinal hernia. (For more information about the use of modifiers, refer to *Coding with Modifiers: A Guide to Correct CPT® and HCPCS Level II Modifier Usage* published by AMA Press.)

When a procedure or service that is designated as a separate procedure is carried out independently or considered to be unrelated or distinct from other procedures or services provided at that time, the procedure or service designated as a separate procedure may be reported by itself, or in addition to other procedures or services by appending modifier 59 (Distinct Procedural Service) to the specific separate procedure code reported. This indicates that the procedure is not considered a component of another procedure, but is a distinct, independent procedure. This may represent any of the following:

- Different session or patient encounter
- Different site or organ system
- Separate incision or excision
- Separate lesion
- Treatment of a separate injury (or area of injury in extensive injuries)

Integumentary System

The Integumentary System section of the CPT codebook includes a variety of procedures performed on the integumentary system of the entire body. Because this section includes procedures for the whole body, it is important to pay close attention to subsection guidelines and the code descriptors to ensure that the appropriate code is chosen for not only the procedure, but also the correct anatomic area. Various types of procedure codes involve such anatomy as:

- Skin and subcutaneous and accessory structures
- Nails
- Breast

Debridement

The Debridement codes in the CPT code set are intended to be used for debridement procedures performed by surgical techniques chosen at the discretion of the physician. When a physician performs debridement, he or she intends to remove all foreign or dead material, reduce the number of bacteria in the wound, and leave intact the viable tissue.

EXAMPLE

A patient had an infected wound on 15% of his body from a previous injury. The physician debrided the wound.

Code **11000** is reported for the first 10% of body surface and **11001** for the remaining 5% (or a fraction thereof).

CODING TIP

"Each additional 10% of the body surface" is reported for each additional 10% of the body surface *or fraction thereof*. This means that debridement of a full 10% of the body area does not have to be additionally performed to report code **11001**. Rather, code **11001** can be reported for any fraction of 10% of body surface that is additionally debrided.

Paring or Cutting

Only one code from the Paring or Cutting series is reported for the total number of lesions that are pared or cut. Multiple codes should not be reported to equal the number of lesions, as these codes are not cumulative and are not designated as add-on codes.

EXAMPLE

A patient had three thick calluses on the heel of his right foot. The physician performed a paring of all calluses. Only code **11056** is reported for the paring of the three calluses.

Removal of Skin Tags

Removal of skin tags is defined as removal by scissoring or any sharp method, ligature strangulation, electrosurgical destruction, or combination of treatment modalities including chemical and electrocauterization. Codes **11200** and **11201** are reported for removal of skin tags from any area of the body.

EXAMPLE

A patient had 17 skin tags on his back. Since they were of different sizes, the physician cut 10 skin tags off with the surgeon's scissors and destroyed 7 skin tags by electrosurgical means.

Code **11200** is reported for up to 15 skin tags and **11201** for the remaining 2 skin tags, since code **11201** includes any additional lesions, up to 10 additional lesions.

CODING TIP

The total number of toenails debrided is added from one or both feet.

Nails

Codes **11720** and **11721** are for debridement of nails. Code **11720** is reported for debridement of one to five nails and **11721** is for debridement of six or more nails. Only one code should be reported from **11720** and **11721** to describe the number of nails debrided, regardless of which extremity. Code **11721** is not designated as an add-on code.

Lateral Nail View

11719–11765

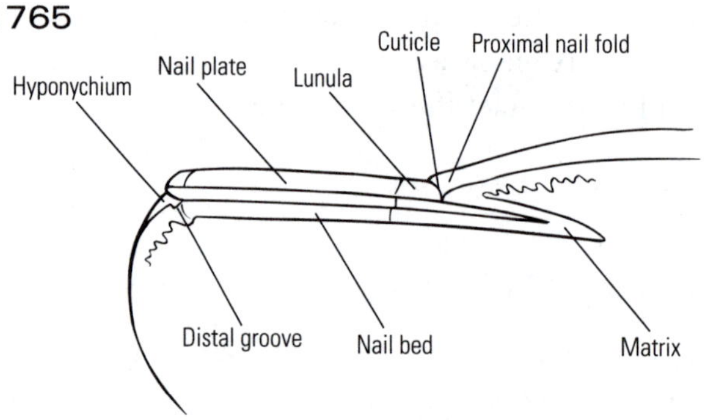

EXAMPLE

A patient had three painful dystrophic toenails on the left foot and three on the right foot. The physician debrided each of the affected nails.

Code **11721** is reported for the debridement of six toenails, three on the left foot and three on the right foot.

Lesions

The CPT code set includes several codes that describe the various techniques used to remove lesions. Codes for shaving, excision, and destruction of lesions can be found throughout the Integumentary System section. To correctly code the removal of lesions, the group of codes that most accurately describes the technique used by the physician should be chosen.

Excision of benign or malignant lesions

Revisions were made to the codes for excision of benign and malignant lesions and their introductory language in *CPT® 2003*. This was done to clarify how these codes should be reported. The definition of *excision* was changed to reflect a full-thickness (through the dermis) removal of a lesion, including margins, and includes simple (nonlayered) closure when performed. Language was added to the guidelines and code descriptors identifying inclusion of the margins as part of the measurement. In addition, the word *lesion* was replaced by *excised diameter* to identify that the measurement is not limited to the lesion size alone. The revised guidelines and code descriptors identify what is included as part of the excision, define what is included as part of the margin, and identify when the measurement is made. Direction for reporting additional excisions and reexcisions(s) is also given.

Excision of benign lesions Each benign lesion excised is reported separately. Code selection is determined by measuring the greatest clinical diameter of the apparent lesion plus that margin required for complete excision (lesion diameter plus the narrowest margins required equals the excised diameter). The margins refer to the narrowest margin required to adequately excise the lesion, based on the physician's judgment. The measurement of lesion plus margins is made before excision. The excised diameter is the same whether the surgical defect is repaired in a linear fashion or reconstructed (eg, with a skin graft). The closure of any defects created by incision, excision, or trauma may require intermediate or complex closure. Any repair by intermediate or complex closure should be reported separately with the appropriate repair codes.

Excision of malignant lesions Each malignant lesion excised is reported separately. Code selection is determined by measuring the greatest clinical diameter of the apparent lesion plus the margin required for complete excision (lesion diameter plus the narrowest margins required equals the excised diameter). The margins refer to the narrowest margin required to adequately excise the lesion, based on the physician's judgment. The measurement of lesion plus margins is made before excision. The excised diameter is the same whether the surgical defect is repaired in a linear fashion or reconstructed (eg, with a skin graft). The closure of any defects created by incision, excision, or trauma may require intermediate or complex closure. Any repair by intermediate or complex closure should be reported separately with the appropriate repair codes. When frozen section pathology shows the margins of excision were not adequate, an additional excision may be necessary for complete tumor removal. Use only one code to report the additional excision and reexcision(s) based on the final widest excised diameter required for complete tumor removal at the same operative session. To report a reexcision procedure performed to widen margins at a subsequent operative session, codes **11600–11646** are used as appropriate. Modifier 58 is appended if the reexcision procedure is performed during the postoperative period of the primary excision procedure.

Repair

The repair of wounds may be classified as simple, intermediate, or complex.

- The simple repair codes are typically used for one-layer closure. Simple repair/closure is included in the excision of a benign or malignant lesion and is not separately reported. Wound closure utilizing adhesive strips as the sole repair material should be coded by means of the appropriate E/M code.
- The *intermediate* repair codes require layered closure of one or more of the deeper layers of subcutaneous tissue and superficial (nonmuscle) fascia, in addition to the skin (epidermal or dermal) closure. These codes are also used for single-layer closure of heavily contaminated wounds that have required extensive cleaning or removal of particulate matter. Intermediate repair does not include excision of benign (**11400–11446**) or malignant (**11600–11646**) lesions.

  It should be noted that that the layered closure involves one or more of the *deeper layers* of subcutaneous tissue and superficial (nonmuscle) fascia, in addition to the skin (epidermal and dermal closure). If a wound is repaired in two layers, but the buried sutures (second layer) do not include at least the deeper layer of subcutaneous tissue, then this is not considered an intermediate repair. In this instance, a simple repair would be reported.
- The *complex* repair codes include repair of wounds requiring more than layered closure, such as scar revision, debridement (eg, traumatic lacerations or avulsions), extensive undermining, stents, or retention sutures. Complex repair does not include excision of benign (**11400–11446**) or malignant (**11600–11646**) lesions.

The repair codes are reported by adding the lengths of the repairs. When multiple wounds are repaired, the lengths of those wounds in the same classification (simple, intermediate, or complex), and from those anatomic sites that are grouped together into the same code descriptor, should be added together and reported as one code.

It is important to note the following:

- The lengths of repairs from different groupings of anatomic sites (eg, face and extremities) are *not* added.
- The lengths of repairs from different classifications (eg, intermediate and complex repairs) are *not* added.

EXAMPLE

After an assault with a knife, a patient required simple repair of a 2-cm laceration of the forehead, intermediate repair of a 3-cm laceration of the neck, simple repair of a 4-cm laceration of the back, simple repair of a 5-cm laceration of the forearm, and complex repair of a 3-cm laceration of the abdomen.

Code **12004** is reported for the simple repair of back and forearm (the two lengths—the back (4 cm) plus the forearm (5 cm)—are included in code **12004**); code **12011** for the simple repair of the forehead; code **12042** for the intermediate repair of the neck; and code **13101** for the complex repair of the abdomen.

Adjacent Tissue Transfer or Rearrangement

Codes **14000–14350** identify adjacent tissue transfer or rearrangement procedures (local flaps). The excision of a lesion, whether it is benign or malignant, is included with these codes. Some examples of tissue transfer/rearrangements include the following:

- Z-plasty
- W-plasty
- V-Y plasty
- Rotation flap
- Advancement flap
- Double pedicle flap

Codes **14000–14350** are reported on the basis of the anatomic area and size. The size refers to the *defect* size, not the lesion size. The term *defect* includes the primary and secondary defects. The primary defect, resulting from the excision, and the secondary defect, resulting from flap design to perform the reconstruction, are measured together to determine the code.

Often the tissue transfer or rearrangement procedure creates an additional defect whose repair must be separately coded. For example, if a skin graft or another flap is necessary to close a secondary defect, this should be reported separately.

EXAMPLE

A patient had a lesion of the right cheek removed, resulting in a primary defect of 10 sq cm. After design, elevation, and mobilization of the rotation flap, a 10 sq cm secondary defect was present. The entire defect resulted in a 20 sq cm defect of the right cheek.

The term defect includes the primary defect from the excision and the secondary defect from the rotation flap. Code **14041** is reported for a total defect of 20 sq cm.

CODING TIP

Procedures are reported on the basis of the size and location of the defect or recipient site.

Free Skin Grafts

A free skin graft is an unattached portion of skin that is transferred to another site. These grafts are reported by the size and location of the lesion, which is the recipient area, and the specific type of graft used. If surgical preparation and management of a burn or wound are necessary, or a recipient site is created by excision of an open wound, burn eschar, or scar, then this is reported separately on the basis of surface area, with the burn and wound preparation and management procedure codes **15000**, **15001**, **15350**, **15351**, **15400**, and **15401**. If the donor site requires repair by a skin graft or flap, then this is reported separately.

EXAMPLE

A patient with multiple healed scars requested that these be removed and repaired for cosmetic purposes. The defects included a 100 sq cm scar of the right cheek and a 200 sq cm defect of the left upper chest. The scar tissue from the defects was cut away, and the sites were prepared for grafting. Several split-thickness skin grafts totaling 300 cm were harvested from the left and right thighs.

Codes reported are **15000** for the right cheek (100 sq cm); **15000** and **15001** for the left upper chest (200 sq cm); **15100** and **15101** for the left upper chest (split-thickness grafts to defect); and **15120** for the right cheek (split-thickness grafts to defect).

Musculoskeletal System

The Musculoskeletal System subsection of Surgery in the CPT codebook is divided by musculoskeletal anatomy. The subsection is further divided by a consistent theme of procedures: incision; excision; introduction or removal; repair, revision, and/or reconstruction; fracture and/or dislocation; arthrodesis; and amputation. This format is repeated throughout the subsection. The codes in the Musculoskeletal System subsection are for the reporting of procedures involving tendons, muscles, fractures and dislocations, spine surgery, bunions, and casting and strapping. Procedures performed via an arthroscope are specifically addressed at the end of the subsection and terms related to the treatment of fractures are included in the introductory language of the Musculoskeletal System subsection in the CPT codebook.

Sections of the Musculoskeletal System are highlighted here along with a review of some basic coding guidelines associated with reporting fractures and dislocations, spine surgery, bunion procedures, and casting and strapping procedures.

Fractures and Dislocations

When fractures and dislocations are reported, it is important to have a clear understanding of the various types of treatment.

Closed treatment

Closed treatment of a fracture or dislocation specifically means that the fracture or dislocation site is not surgically opened. This treatment is used to describe procedures that treat fractures by one of three methods:

- Without manipulation
- With manipulation
- With or without traction

Open treatment

Open treatment means that the fracture is surgically opened and visualized to allow internal fixation.

Percutaneous skeletal fixation

This type of treatment is neither open nor closed. In this procedure, the fracture fragments are not visualized, but fixation (eg, pins) is placed across the fracture site, usually under x-ray imaging.

Manipulation

This term is used in many sections of the CPT codebook. The definition used here applies to codes in the Musculoskeletal System section. Manipulation is the attempted reduction or restoration of a fracture or joint dislocation to its normal anatomic alignment by applying forces.

Injections

The Musculoskeletal System section includes codes to report injections into tendon sheaths, ligaments, muscles, and trigger points. Code **20550** is used to report single or multiple injections per single anatomic tendon sheath, ligament, or aponeurosis. Code **20551** is used to report single or multiple injections per single tendon origin/insertion. When multiple injections to the *same* tendon are performed, they are reported only once. When injections to *multiple* tendon sheaths, ligaments, tendon origins, or tendon insertions are performed, they are reported one time for each injection.

The codes for trigger point injections, codes **20552** and **20553**, are intended to be reported once per session, regardless of the number of trigger points or muscles injected. Whenever radiological imaging guidance is performed in addition to the injection procedures, the appropriate radiology codes (**76003**, **76393**, **76942**) should be reported in addition to the injection codes to describe the imaging guidance.

Spine Surgery

When coding for spine surgery, the coder must consider and apply various guidelines that are included in the beginning of the Spine subsection in the CPT codebook. These guidelines include various coding components such as bone grafting, arthrodesis, and spinal instrumentation. Careful review of these instructions along with each code descriptor is also imperative to ensure that the correct codes are selected.

It is important to understand various anatomic terms when spine surgeries are coded. Important terms include the following:

- **Types of vertebrae**: cervical, thoracic, lumbar, sacral
- **Interspace**: the nonbony compartment between two adjacent vertebral bodies that contains the intervertebral disk and includes the nucleus pulposus, annulus fibrosus, and two cartilaginous endplates
- **Segment**: the basic constituent part into which the spine may be divided. It represents a single complete vertebral bone with its associated articular processes and laminae
- **Vertebral components**: the vertebral body, spinous process, laminae, facets, and intervertebral disk
- **Arthrodesis**: Surgical fusion/fixation of a joint
- **Segmental instrumentation**: Fixation at each end of the construct and at least one additional interposed bony attachment
- **Nonsegmental instrumentation**: Fixation at each end of the construct, possibly spanning several vertebral segments without attachment to the intervening segments

Sometimes, spinal procedures include reporting codes from the Nervous System subsection in addition to codes from the Musculoskeletal System subsection for reporting various procedures such as laminectomy and spinal cord decompression.

When multiple surgeons act as primary surgeons on the basis of the complexity of the procedure(s), modifier 62 can be appended to certain appropriate codes to reflect that surgeons worked together as primary surgeons. Modifier 62 may not be appended to the spinal instrumentation codes and spinal bone graft codes.

Bunion Procedures

Coding for the correction of a bunion and its associated deformities can be challenging. Not all bunion deformities are the same, and different techniques are needed to repair different levels of deformity. A common deformity of the first metatarsophalangeal (MTP) joint is a hallux valgus (bunion). The CPT code set includes codes for reporting various techniques used to correct bunion deformities.

All of the codes in the **28290–28299** series include integral components when performed at the first MTP joint. The following procedures, therefore, are not reported separately:

- Capsulotomy
- Arthrotomy
- Synovial biopsy
- Neuroplasty
- Synovectomy
- Tendon release
- Tenotomy
- Tenolysis

- Excision of medial eminence
- Excision of associated osteophytes
- Placement of internal fixation
- Scar revision
- Articular shaving
- Removal of bursal tissue

Mitchell Procedure
28296

A complex, biplanar, double step-cut osteotomy through the neck of the first metatarsal. Also called Mitchell Chevron (Austin) procedure.

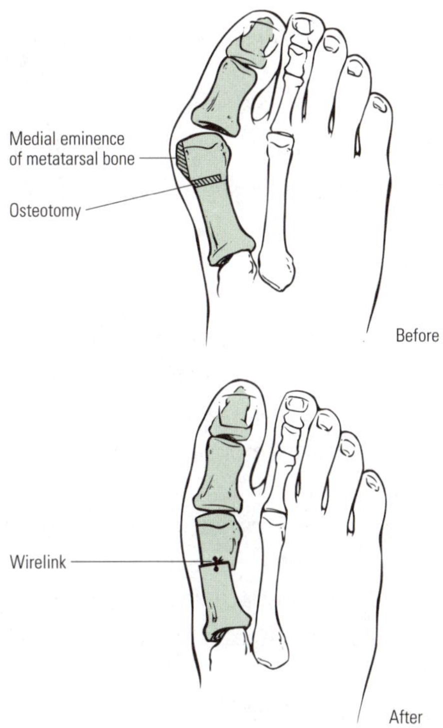

Application of Casts and Strapping

The guidelines at the beginning of the Musculoskeletal System subsection in the CPT codebook indicate that the services listed in this subsection include the application and removal of the first cast or traction device only. Subsequent replacement of a cast and/or traction device may require an additional listing with the **29000–29799** series of codes from the Application of Casts and Strapping subsection. These codes have specific guidelines pertaining to their use. It is important to develop a good understanding of these guidelines to appropriately code for the application of casts and strapping. Application of casts and strapping may be reported for:

- A replacement cast or strapping procedure, during or after the period of normal follow-up care

- An initial service performed without restorative treatment or procedures, to stabilize or protect a fracture, injury, or dislocation, and/or to relieve pain
- An initial cast or strapping service when no other treatment or procedure is performed or expected to be performed by the same physician
- An initial cast or strapping service when another physician provides a restorative treatment or procedure(s)

There are two questions to consider before reporting an initial cast or strapping with a casting and strapping code:

1 Will any restorative treatment or procedure(s) (eg, surgical repair, closed or open reduction of a fracture or joint dislocation) be performed, or is treatment expected to be performed?

2 Will the same physician assume all subsequent fracture, dislocation, or injury care?

Answering these questions will assist in establishing a good basis for deciding whether the casts and strapping codes should be reported.

Endoscopy/Arthroscopy

Codes **29800–29999** are used to report endoscopic and arthroscopic musculoskeletal procedures. The guidelines at the beginning of this category of codes in the CPT codebook indicate that surgical arthroscopy always includes a diagnostic arthroscopy, as the diagnostic arthroscopy is considered an integral component of surgical arthroscopy.

General guidelines for coding endoscopic and arthroscopic procedures are as follows:

- The coder should look up endoscopy, arthroscopy, or laparoscopy in the index and locate the organ or system being examined or treated with a scope.
- The codes in that system/organ section should be reviewed to find an endoscopy, arthroscopy, or laparoscopy heading.
- If there is no endoscopy, arthroscopy, or laparoscopy heading in that section, a code with a descriptor that includes the suffix "oscopy" and describes the procedure performed should be selected.
- If there is no heading for endoscopy, arthroscopy, or laparoscopy, or there is *not* a specific code mentioning the use of an endoscope in its descriptor, the codes described in that section are for "open" surgical procedures and *should not* be used to report a procedure using an endoscopic approach.
- The physician should be asked to clarify that the procedure was performed with an endoscope or laparoscope.
- If there is not a specific code for the endoscopy/arthroscopy/laparoscopy procedure in question, the unlisted procedure code in the Endoscopy/Arthroscopy subsection is used to report the procedure. When an unlisted code is reported, a copy of the operative report should be submitted to the insurance company when the claim is filed.

Respiratory System

The Respiratory System subsection is divided into the following anatomic sites:

- Nose
- Accessory sinuses
- Larynx
- Trachea and bronchi
- Lungs and pleura

Consistent with other subsections of the CPT codebook, the Respiratory System also includes an Endoscopy subheading for each anatomic site, where an endoscopic approach is applicable. Surgical endoscopy always includes diagnostic endoscopy when performed by the same physician.

Trachea and Bronchi

A bronchoscopy is reported with a code(s) in the **31622–31656** series. Bronchoscopy is considered an inherently bilateral procedure. All of the codes in the **31622–31646** series include fluoroscopic guidance when performed. Therefore, a separate code would not be reported for fluoroscopy used in conjunction with bronchoscopy.

Different codes are available to describe various procedures performed via bronchoscopy. These include three distinctly different types of biopsies that are performed via bronchoscopy:

- **Bronchial mucosal biopsies (31625),** which are taken by direct vision and can be reported only once, even if performed at different anatomic sites
- **Transbronchial lung biopsies (31628),** which are lung biopsies taken peripherally with fluoroscopic guidance of the biopsy forceps and, importantly, when taken from different lobes, which represent new procedures with independent risk factors, including biopsy forceps location of the lesion, bleeding, pneumothorax, air embolism, etc
- **Transbronchial needle aspiration biopsies (31629),** which are taken centrally by penetration of a large airway with a specially designed biopsy needle and aspiration of a lymph node or central mass lesion. This represents a less invasive approach than invasive surgical biopsy, with the attendant additional risks of an open procedure.

Add-on code **31632** is intended to describe performance of transbronchial lung biopsy in each additional lobe and **31633** to describe the needle aspiration biopsies in each additional lobe after the initial lobar needle aspiration procedure. While these codes may be reported for each biopsy in a separate lobe, parenthetical instructions direct the coder that it would be inappropriate to report multiple biopsies or aspirations within the same lobe. Some possible sites for a bronchoscopic biopsy include the upper airway, which extends from the vocal cords to the lobar bronchi; each of the five lobes of the lungs and their bronchi; the right upper, middle, and lower lobes; and the left upper and lower lobes.

Bronchoscopy
31622–31656

A rigid or flexible bronchoscope is inserted through the oropharynx, vocal cords, and beyond the trachea into the right/left bronchi.

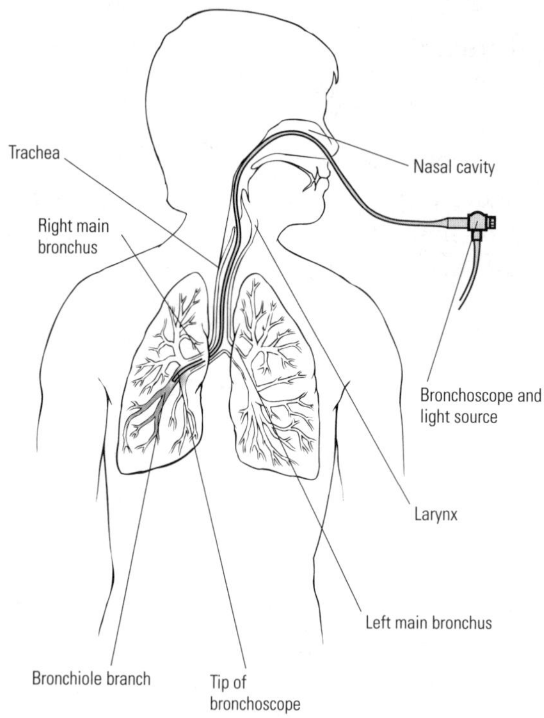

Cardiovascular System

The Cardiovascular System subsection of the CPT codebook contains codes for reporting procedures of the heart and pericardium, arteries, and veins. The focus of this section of Chapter 3 is on the guidelines associated with pacemaker and defibrillator procedures and coronary artery bypass procedures.

Pacemaker or Pacing Cardioverter-Defibrillator

A pacemaker system includes a pulse generator (containing electronics and a battery) and one or more electrodes (leads). The pulse generator is placed in a subcutaneous "pocket" created either in an infraclavicular site or underneath the abdominal muscles just below the rib cage. Electrodes (leads) may be inserted through a vein (transvenous) or placed on the surface of the heart (epicardial). Epicardial placement of electrodes requires a thoracotomy or sternotomy.

In addition to the various placement methods, different types of systems may be inserted. A single-chamber pacemaker system includes a pulse generator and one electrode inserted in either the atrium or the right ventricle. A dual-chamber pacemaker system involves the insertion of electrodes into both the atrium and the right ventricle that are then connected to a pulse generator capable of pacing and sensing both the atrium and the ventricle.

Biventricular pacing systems are used when pacing of the left ventricle is required, in addition to pacing of the right ventricle. The implant procedure for the biventricular system is similar to that of a single- or dual-chamber system, with the additional complexity of the transvenous placement of the lead in a cardiac vein to reach the left ventricle. Implantation of a biventricular system requires a coronary guide catheter and the use of venography to guide the lead through the coronary sinus and into a cardiac vein for placement in the left ventricle.

Pacing Cardioverter-Defibrillator Systems

The combination pacing cardioverter-defibrillator device is designed to recognize and provide antitachycardia pacing, dual-chamber bradycardia therapy, and atrial and/or ventricular defibrillation therapy. A pacing cardioverter-defibrillator system may be inserted in a single chamber (pacing in the right ventricle), in dual chambers (pacing in the atrium and ventricle), or as a biventricular system (pacing in the left and right ventricles). In addition to implantation of a pulse generator, pacing cardioverter-defibrillators may require multiple lead insertions, even when only a single chamber is being paced. Pacing cardioverter-defibrillator pulse generators may be implanted in a subcutaneous infraclavicular pocket or in an abdominal pocket. Removal of a pacing cardioverter-defibrillator pulse generator requires opening of the existing subcutaneous pocket and disconnecting the pulse generator from its electrode(s). A thoracotomy (or laparotomy in the case of abdominally placed generators) is not required to remove the pulse generator.

When the "battery" of a pacemaker or pacing cardioverter-defibrillator is changed, it is actually the pulse generator that is replaced. A code for the removal of the pulse generator and a separate code for the insertion of the new generator are reported for the replacement.

If removal and replacement procedures are performed, then both procedures are reported separately. In most circumstances, the electrodes of a pacing cardioverter-defibrillator system are positioned in the heart transvenously. Electrode positioning on the epicardial surface of the heart requires a thoracotomy or sternotomy and is reported with codes **33245** and **33246**. Removal of the electrode(s) may first be attempted by transvenous extraction, described by code **33244**. If transvenous extraction is unsuccessful, a thoracotomy may be required to remove the electrodes (as described by code **33243**). Replacement of a pacemaker electrode, pacing cardioverter-defibrillator electrode(s), or a left ventricular pacing electrode is reported with codes **33206–33208**, **33210–33213**, or **33224**. Repositioning of a pacemaker electrode, pacing cardioverter-defibrillator electrode(s), or left ventricular pacing electrode is reported with code **33215** or **33226**.

Coronary Artery Bypass Procedures

Venous grafting or arterial grafting

Coronary artery bypass graft procedures may be reported in three ways, depending on the type of operation performed. The first two reporting methods require only a single code:

- A bypass operation performed with only venous grafts. This is reported with a single code from the **33510–33516** series, reflecting the number of distal anastomoses performed.
- A bypass operation performed with only internal mammary arteries or other arteries. This is reported with a single code from the **33533–33536** series, with code selection again reflecting the number of distal anastomoses performed. The codes in this series are also used to report coronary artery bypass procedures with a combination of arterial and venous grafts.

Coronary Artery Bypass—Venous Grafting Only
33510–33516

A. Use 33510 to report a single coronary venous graft.

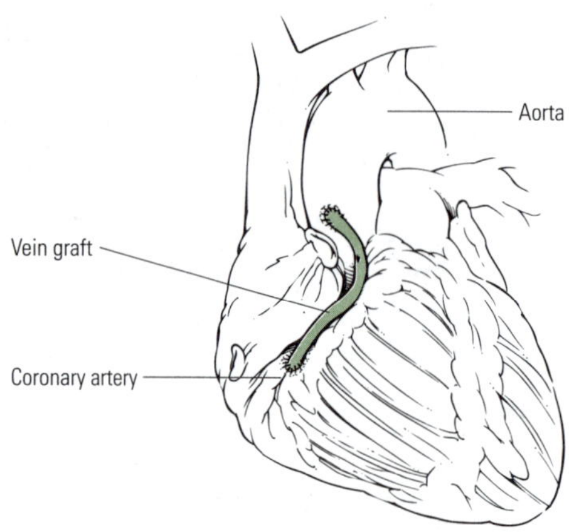

B. Report 33512 when three coronary venous grafts are performed.

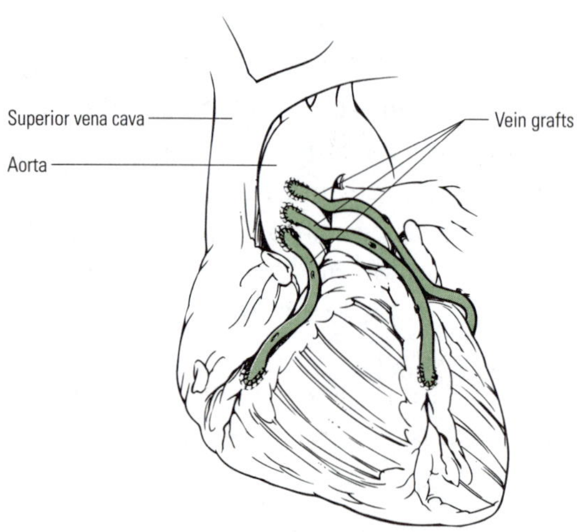

The third reporting method requires the use of two codes:

- A code to indicate that both arteries and veins were used (from the **33517–33523** series). The appropriate code should describe the number of distal venous anastomoses used for the bypass
- An arterial graft code to indicate the number of distal arterial anastomoses required for the bypass procedure (from the **33533–33536** series)

Codes in the Combined Arterial-Venous Grafting for Coronary Bypass series are not to be reported alone. The appropriate vein graft code from this series is used in conjunction with a code from the arterial grafting series to completely describe combined arterial-venous grafting for coronary bypass. As indicated by the symbol placed before each code, codes **33517–33523** are exempt from the use of modifier 51.

Open Procurement of Graft Material

Open procurement of the saphenous vein graft is included in the description of work for the venous grafting and combined arterial-venous grafting for coronary artery bypass codes and should not be reported as a separate service or cosurgery. Additionally, arterial graft procurement is included in the description of work for the arterial grafting for coronary artery bypass codes and should not be reported as a separate service or cosurgery.

Open procurement of these three types of graft material is reported separately:

- Upper extremity vein (**+35500**)
- Femoropopliteal vein (**+35572**)
- Upper extremity artery (**35600**)

The procurement of these vessels for graft material requires additional decision making and more technically difficult surgical work. These procedures may be indicated for patients who, for example, have had previous bypass surgery or severe vascular disease, resulting in a lack of suitable superficial autogenous vessels for graft material. Codes **35500** and **35572** are designated as add-on codes and are not reported alone. Additionally, codes **33517–33523** are designated as modifier 51 exempt and therefore should not have modifier 51 appended to any of them.

Redo Operations

CPT code **33530** is an add-on code used to report coronary artery bypass or valve reoperation procedures performed more than one month after the original operation. It is not reported alone, but is reported in addition to the appropriate code(s) to describe the bypass or valve procedure performed.

Repeat sternotomy requires removal of previously placed wire sutures, which sometimes become embedded in the bony portion of the sternum. Because the anterior cardiac chambers, great vessels, and other mediastinal structures may be densely adherent to the posterior table of the sternum, the sternal incision must be made with extreme care to avoid potential hemorrhage. Once the mediastinum has been entered, the scarring and adhesions from previous surgery usually obscure the anatomic landmarks and make dissection both difficult and hazardous. Therefore, code **33530** is reported to reflect the increased difficulty associated with the redo procedure.

When a redo coronary artery bypass procedure is reported, only the number and type of bypass grafts used in the redo procedure are reported. Procedures from the first operation are not reported for redos.

Digestive System

In the Digestive System section of the CPT codebook, codes exist for reporting endoscopy procedures. The types of endoscopy procedures include:

- Esophagoscopy
- Esophagogastroduodenoscopy
- Endoscopic retrograde cholangiopancreatography
- Enteroscopy
- Proctosigmoidoscopy
- Sigmoidoscopy
- Colonoscopy
- Anoscopy

Esophagoscopy is limited to study of the esophagus. When the endoscope passes the diaphragm into the stomach, the procedure is an esophagogastroscopy. When the pyloric channel is traversed, it is described as an esophagogastroduodenoscopy. Enteroscopy, or small intestinal endoscopy, is the examination of the small intestine beyond the second portion of the duodenum. Endoscopic retrograde cholangiopancreatography is the examination of the hepatobiliary system and gallbladder. Proctosigmoidoscopy is the examination of the rectum and sigmoid colon. Sigmoidoscopy is the examination of the entire rectum and sigmoid colon and may include examination of a portion of the descending colon. Colonoscopy describes an endoscopy in which a colonoscope is inserted in the anus and moved through the colon proximally past the splenic flexure (meaning the examiner is able to advance the colonoscope beyond the splenic flexure) to visualize the lumen of the transverse and ascending colon (right side) to the cecum and/or terminal ileum.

When the endoscopy procedures are reported, it is important to remember that surgical endoscopy *always* includes diagnostic endoscopy. Also, when two distinct endoscopic procedures are performed on the same day or at the same session, it is appropriate to report these procedures separately.

EXAMPLE

An esophagogastroduodenoscopy with biopsy (**43239**) and an esophagogastroduodenoscopy with dilation of gastric outlet for obstruction (**43245**) are performed. The physician reports the codes as follows:

43245
43239-51

In this case, both codes are reported to completely describe the procedures performed. The primary procedure is reported without the use of a modifier. Modifier 51 is appended to the secondary procedure performed. Modifier 51 is also used to report multiple procedures (other than E/M services) performed at the same session by the same provider.

CODING TIP

Several endoscopic procedures listed in the CPT codebook are available for reporting endoscopic control of bleeding by any method. These codes are intended to be used when treatment is required to control bleeding that occurs spontaneously, or as a result of traumatic injury (noniatrogenic), and not as a result of another type of operative intervention. For example, if a sigmoidoscopy with endoscopic biopsy is performed, and the excision of the tissue specimen causes bleeding that is controlled endoscopically, this would be reported only with code **45331** (for the sigmoidoscopy with biopsy). In this case, it is incorrect to report code **45334** (sigmoidoscopy with control of bleeding) to describe the situation, because any control of iatrogenically caused bleeding is included in the biopsy procedure.

Urinary System

The Urinary System subsection of the CPT codebook contains codes for reporting procedures of the kidneys, ureters, bladder, and urethra. Generally, under each anatomic heading, codes can be found for reporting procedures involving incision, excision, introduction, repair, and endoscopy procedures.

Endoscopy Procedures

Some of the most frequently used procedures listed in the Urinary System subsection of the CPT codebook are endoscopic, including the use of cystoscopy, urethroscopy, cystourethroscopy, ureteroscopy, pyeloscopy, and renal endoscopy. An endoscopy can be used as a diagnostic tool performed before proceeding with a more intensive surgical procedure, or to check on the progress, completion, or a complication during the surgical procedure.

CPT descriptors indicate whether an endoscopic procedure is included in the surgical procedure. Examples of the use of cystourethroscopy before, during, or after a urological procedure include a sling operation for stress incontinence (code **57288**), to check status of sutures in the bladder, or transperineal placement of needles or catheters into the prostate (code **55859**), to check for radioactive seeds that may have become dislodged during the procedure. The use of cystourethroscopy in these examples would not be reported separately.

There are times, however, when one endoscopic procedure must be performed before a more extensive endoscopic procedure because of anatomic locations. In this case, the modifier 51 is appended to indicate that multiple procedures were performed at the same session by the same provider.

EXAMPLE

A patient presented for a cystourethroscopy and removal of a calculus located in the ureter. However, to remove the calculus, the urethral stricture must be dilated to provide access. Codes **52352** Cystourethroscopy, with ureteroscopy and/or pyeloscopy; with removal or manipulation of calculus (ureteral catheterization is included), and **52281-51**

Cystourethroscopy, with calibration and/or dilation of urethral stricture or stenosis, with or without meatotomy, with or without injection procedure for cystography, male or female, are reported.

Laterality

Cystourethroscopy codes that are inherently unilateral are **52005**, **52007**, and **52320–52355**, excluding **52347**.

When unilateral procedures are performed bilaterally, the modifier 50 should be appended to the appropriate code(s). (For Medicare purposes only, code **52005** is inherently bilateral; therefore modifier 50 is not appended to code **52005** for Medicare reporting. When code **52005** is reported for non-Medicare purposes, modifier 50 should be appended for bilateral procedures.)

Cystourethroscopy codes that should never be reported with modifier 50 are **52000**, **52010**, **52204–52285**, **52305–52318**, and **52347**.

Code **52351** is not routinely reported with codes **52341–52346** and **52352–52355**, as it describes a diagnostic cystourethroscopy when performed on the same side. However, there are instances when a diagnostic cystourethroscopy and a procedure described by a code from the **52341–52346** or **52352–52355** series are performed on contralateral (opposite) sides of the body. When this is performed, code **52351** is reported separately with modifier 59 appended.

Prostate Procedures

Codes in the **52450–52700** series are used to report transurethral procedures of the vesical neck and prostate. Codes **53850–53853** are also used to report transurethral destruction of prostatic tissue.

Code **52601** is used to report a procedure commonly referred to as *TURP* (transurethral resection of the prostate). This procedure uses electrical current to heat a wire loop on a resectoscope that slices through urethral or prostatic tissue like a knife. Two settings exist to regulate the current: high-voltage current is used to cut the tissue and low-voltage current to coagulate the bleeding. As indicated in the code descriptor, when code **52601** is reported, vasectomy, meatotomy, cystourethroscopy, urethral calibration and/or dilation, and internal urethrotomy are included, when performed, and not reported separately. This code is intended to describe an initial resection of the prostate as well as a complete TURP.

Prostate resection can be performed in two stages. Code **52612** is used to report the first stage of a two-stage resection. Code **52614** describes the second stage of a two-stage resection procedure and is reported when the resection is completed.

Other procedures involving the prostate include noncontact laser coagulation (**52647**), contact laser vaporization (**52648**), transurethral microwave thermotherapy (**53850**), transurethral destruction by radiofrequency thermotherapy (**53852**), and transurethral destruction of prostate tissue by water-induced thermotherapy (**53853**).

Code **52647** describes noncontact laser coagulation of the prostate. This code is intended to describe laser procedures that primarily heat the prostate and require sloughing for the treatment to be complete. This code is reported even if an incision or small amount of vaporization is done in combination with the coagulation. In this case, it is not appropriate to separately report code **52648** for the small amount of vaporization performed. Code **52648** describes contact laser vaporization with or without transurethral resection of the prostate. This code is used to report laser procedures that use a contact tip or high-power density. Contact vaporization is usually accomplished by moving a laser tip across the surface of the prostate, causing immediate vaporization of tissue and an end result that looks like a cavity (similar to the effect of a TURP).

Code **53850** describes transurethral microwave thermotherapy, which is the selective destruction of prostate cells by therapeutic levels of heating. Transurethral microwave thermotherapy is a process of delivering sufficient microwave heating to destroy prostatic tissue without causing unnecessary damage to surrounding structures. The technique combines the principles of microwave radiative heating and conductive cooling to destroy tissue deep within the prostate, while preserving surrounding structures such as the bladder neck, urethral mucosa, and distal sphincter.

Code **53852** describes transurethral destruction by radiofrequency thermotherapy, where low-power radiofrequency energy is used to cause tissue ablation and coagulation of prostate tissue. Insulated needles are pierced through the prostatic urethra to deliver radiofrequency energy directly into the prostate while the insulation on the needles protects the urethra. This procedure creates areas of necrosis within the prostate while preserving the urethral tissue.

Code **53853** describes transurethral destruction of prostate tissue by water-induced thermotherapy, where water is heated outside the body and circulated through the prostate in heat-shielded catheters; only the balloon emits heat. At 60°C, coagulative necrosis of the prostatic tissue occurs to an average depth of 1.0 cm from the urethra. As water is heated and pumped from outside the body, there is no need to use internal temperature probes, as is necessary with benign prostatic hypertrophy treatments, such as microwave (code **53850**) and radiofrequency-based (code **53852**) procedures.

Female Genital System

The Female Genital System subsection includes codes for reporting procedures on the vulva, perineum, and introitus (codes **56405–56821**); vagina (**57000–57425**); cervix uteri (codes **57452–57820**); corpus uteri (codes **58100–58579**); oviduct/ovary (codes **58600–58770**); ovary (codes **58800–58960**); and in vitro fertilization (codes **58970–58976**). Definitions for simple, radical, partial, and complete vulvectomy are included under the Vulva, Perineum, and Introitus heading of the CPT codebook. They are:

- **Simple vulvectomy:** Removal of skin and superficial subcutaneous tissues
- **Radical vulvectomy:** Removal of skin and deep subcutaneous tissue
- **Partial vulvectomy:** Removal of less than 80% of the vulvar area
- **Complete vulvectomy:** Removal of greater than 80% of the vulva

Various hysterectomy procedures are described under the heading Corpus Uteri. The extent of the procedure performed should be clearly documented in the operative report. Removal of the fallopian tube(s) and/or ovary(s) when performed with an abdominal hysterectomy procedure is not reported separately, as the code descriptors for abdominal hysterectomy procedures include the language "with or without removal of tube(s), with or without removal of ovary(s)." In addition, if an enterocele or urethrocystopexy repair is performed at the same session as a vaginal hysterectomy procedure, it should be determined whether the appropriate codes in the **58260–58294** series are available before referring to procedures from the **57200–57330** series of codes.

Maternity Care and Delivery

The services normally provided in uncomplicated maternity cases include antepartum care, delivery, and postpartum care. This is the global package for maternity care and delivery. The guidelines at the beginning of the Maternity Care and Delivery subsection define the services included when antepartum care, delivery services, and postpartum care are reported. Antepartum care includes the initial and subsequent history; physical examinations; recording of weight, blood pressures, and fetal heart tones; routine chemical urinalysis; monthly visits up to 28 weeks' gestation; biweekly visits to 36 weeks' gestation; and weekly visits until delivery. The E/M services (visits) provided with those services included in the provision of antepartum care are not separately reported. However, any other visits or services provided within the antepartum period, other than those listed above, should be coded and reported separately.

Global Services for Routine Obstetric Care

When the same physician (solo practice) or same physician group (group practice) provides the global routine obstetric care (including antepartum care, delivery, and postpartum care), the appropriate global code is reported to describe the services rendered. Codes **59400**, **59510**, **59610**, and **59618** describe the global services for routine obstetric care. Under certain circumstances, the same physician (in a solo practice) or same physician group (group practice) does not provide the global maternity care and delivery services. Under these circumstances, the use of the global codes is not appropriate. Codes in the CPT codebook exist for reporting the specific services provided when the global codes are not appropriate. Codes **59425** and **59426** are available for reporting antepartum care only. Codes **59409**, **59514**, **59612**, and **59620** describe delivery services only. Codes **59410**, **59515**, **59614**, and **59622** describe delivery services including postpartum care. The provision of postpartum care only is reported with code **59430**.

Nervous System

The Nervous System subsection describes diagnostic and therapeutic procedures on the following areas:

- The central nervous system, comprising the brain and spinal cord
- The peripheral nervous system, controlling nerves that relay and receive messages connecting the central nervous system and other body parts
- The autonomic nervous system, controlling involuntary functions of internal organs

Consistent with the communication network of the nervous system anatomy, the Nervous System subsection attempts to list procedures in an anatomic head-to-toe or brain-to-peripheral nerves format. However, from a procedural perspective, a strict anatomic separation is not entirely possible, as certain procedures inherently affect communication and coordination of information to and from the central nervous system (brain and spinal cord) and the peripheral nervous system (voluntary and autonomic systems). It is important to become familiar with the medical terminology and differentiation of intracranial vs extracranial anatomy to appropriately use these codes.

Skull, Meninges, and Brain

Twist drill, burr hole(s), or trephine

Codes **61000–61070** describe diagnostic or therapeutic injection, drainage, or aspiration procedures. These codes do not include imaging guidance. When it is performed, the appropriate imaging guidance code from the Radiology section should be additionally reported.

Craniectomy or craniotomy

The **61304–61576** series of codes describe craniotomy and craniectomy procedures involving various surgical approaches through the skull to reach a specific area of the brain because of disease or trauma (eg, **61546**), or for reconstructive procedures related to congenital or acquired defect (eg, **61556**). Anatomic landmarks and approaches may assist in choosing the best codes. For example, excision of a cerebellopontine angle tumor of the infratentorial or posterior fossa is reported with code **61520**, as opposed to excision of a cerebellopontine angle tumor (ie, acoustic neuroma) involving a transtemporal craniectomy/bone flap craniotomy, reported by code **61526**. If harvest of graft material requiring separate incision is performed, this should be additionally reported by means of the appropriate graft code. Some of the craniotomy procedures (**61340**, **61490**) may be performed unilaterally or bilaterally, depending on the involved anatomy. If a bilateral procedure is performed, then modifier 50 should be appended to the appropriate code.

Surgery of skull base

Skull base surgery can be performed as the initial treatment for lesions of the base of the skull or to excise a lesion after the initial surgery to excise a lesion has failed because of recurrence of the initial tumor. Coding for skull base procedures requires a thorough understanding of anatomy of the brain and adjoining structures, a good anatomy and physiology text, and a medical dictionary.

Guidelines for use of codes for surgery of skull base The format of the skull base procedures is based on the division of the cranium into anterior, middle, and posterior fossae. For each of these anatomic regions, codes were developed that describe the surgical approach, definitive procedure, and defect reconstruction. Within this format, any number of surgeons can use the appropriate codes for their specific role in the overall treatment of a patient with a cranial base lesion.

Surgical management of lesions involving the skull base often requires the skills of several surgeons of varying specialties, working together or in tandem during the operative session. These operations are single-staged and require primary closure of the surgical defect to avoid life-threatening infectious complications such as meningitis and osteomyelitis. The procedures are categorized according to:

- Approach procedure necessary to obtain adequate exposure to the lesion
- Definitive procedure(s) necessary to biopsy, excise, or otherwise treat the lesion
- Reconstruction/repair of the defect present after the definitive procedure(s)

When a single surgeon performs the approach procedure, another performs the definitive procedure, and a third surgeon performs the reconstruction/repair procedure, each surgeon reports only the CPT code number and descriptor for the specific procedure performed. If one surgeon performs more than one procedure (ie, approach and definitive procedure), then both CPT codes are reported, with modifier 51 appended to the secondary additional procedure(s). However, add-on procedures cannot be performed if the basic procedure was not performed. Therefore, modifier 51 should not be appended to the add-on codes.

Stereotaxis

Codes **61720–61793** describe intracranial procedures utilizing a unique radiologic guidance/localization method, namely, stereotaxis. In certain cases, mounting of a stereotactic head frame is an integral part of the proposed procedure when performed. Therefore, the application or removal of the stereotactic frame, code **20660**, is not additionally reported unless performed as a "separate procedure" on a date before the procedure by the same or a different physician. Stereotactic radiosurgery, code **61793**, includes the phrase "one or more sessions." This refers to performing stereotactic radiosurgery on a single lesion. However, if two lesions are being treated, then code **61793** would be reported twice.

Neurostimulators (intracranial)

The Neurostimulators (Intracranial) codes (**61850–61888**) are for deep brain stimulation. These codes describe procedures targeting sites where electrodes can be applied for:

- Stimulation
- The radiologic technology (computer-guided magnetic resonance imaging or computed tomographic stereotactic elements) necessary for placement of these electrode arrays
- The technique or approach used to implant the neurostimulator components (ie, electrodes or pulse generator)

When microelectrode recording is performed by the operating surgeon, in association with implantation of neurostimulator electrode arrays, it is an inclusive service and should not be reported separately. If another physician participates in neurophysiologic mapping during a deep brain stimulator implantation procedure, this service may be reported by the other physician with code **95961** or **95962**.

Spine and Spinal Cord

The Spine and Spinal Cord codes, **62263–63746**, include various procedures such as spinal injection, drainage, or aspiration; catheter implantation; and reservoir/pump implantation. Also included are procedures such as posterior extradural laminotomy or laminectomy for exploration or decompression of neural elements or excision of herniated intervertebral disks, as well as spinal neurostimulators.

Extracranial Nerves, Peripheral Nerves, and Autonomic Nervous System

This section includes codes for injection of an anesthetic agent (nerve block) for diagnostic or therapeutic purposes. These injections include the somatic and sympathetic nerves. Codes **64400–64450** are differentiated by single injections, multiple injections, or continuous infusion, with codes **64416**, **64446**, and **64448** describing continuous catheter infusions to the brachial plexus, sciatic nerve, and femoral nerve after the insertion of an infusion catheter into the sheaths of nerves. The services provided for daily management of continuous anesthetic administration to the brachial plexus, sciatic nerve, and femoral nerve are included in these codes and therefore not separately reported.

The paravertebral facet joint or facet joint nerve codes (**64470–64476**) specify the spinal anatomy, the substances injected, and the spinal level or levels involved. Codes **64470–64476** are considered unilateral procedures. When injections are performed at both right and left paravertebral facet joints or paravertebral facet joint nerves, the bilateral procedure modifier 50 is appended to the appropriate code. Although not specifically stated in the descriptor nomenclature, injection of contrast material is considered an inclusive component of codes **64470–64476** and therefore not reported separately. The paravertebral facet joint or paravertebral facet joint nerve injections (**64470–64476**) are performed under fluoroscopic guidance for precise anatomic localization to avoid potential intrusion of the vertebral artery or damage to the spinal cord or surrounding nerve roots. Code **76005** for fluoroscopic guidance and localization is not an inclusive component of codes **64470–64476** and therefore should be additionally reported.

Transforaminal epidural spinal injection technique is a technically different approach from central epidural injection. Because the vertebral artery as well as the spinal cord is close to the nerve root, this procedural technique is more difficult than a central epidural injection. Codes **64479–64484** identify the spinal anatomy, the substances injected, and the spinal level or levels involved. Codes **64480** and **64484** represent add-on codes for each additional spinal level injected. Codes **64479–64484** are considered unilateral procedures. When both right and left transforaminal epidural injections are performed, the bilateral procedure modifier 50 is appended to the appropriate code. Similar to the paravertebral facet joint or paravertebral facet joint nerve injections, transforaminal epidural spinal injections are also performed under fluoroscopic guidance for precise anatomic localization to avoid potential intrusion of the vertebral artery or damage to the spinal cord or surrounding nerve roots. Code **76005** for fluoroscopic guidance and localization is not an inclusive component of codes **64479–64484** and should be additionally reported.

Destruction by neurolytic agent (eg, chemical, thermal, electrical, or radiofrequency)

Although this heading includes codes for reporting destruction by neurolytic agent to somatic and sympathetic nerves, the term *destruction* does not apply to all of the **64600–64640** series of codes. Destruction does not apply to codes **64612–64614**, as the nerve is technically not destroyed but is *chemodenervated*, meaning that the effect of the drug injection (eg, type A botulinum toxin) is largely or completely reversible. To innervate muscles of the limb or trunk muscles, botulinum toxin is injected directly into the muscle through an electrode to treat dystonia, spasticity, cerebral palsy, multiple sclerosis, muscle spasms, spinal cord injuries, and multiple sclerosis. Codes **64612–64614** are reported once, even though multiple injections are performed in sites along a particular muscle (several muscles are typically injected). Code **64999** Unlisted procedure, nervous system, is used if the botulinum toxin injection(s) is performed on a muscle(s) not specified in these codes.

The codes for destruction by neurolytic agent, paravertebral facet joint nerve (**64622–64627**), are considered unilateral procedures. When both right-side and left-side injections are performed, the bilateral procedure modifier 50 is appended to the appropriate code. Fluoroscopic guidance and localization are performed to assist in accurately localizing specific spinal anatomy for placement of a needle or catheter tip for spinal or paraspinous diagnostic or therapeutic injection procedures. Since fluoroscopic guidance and localization is not an inclusive component of codes **64622–64627**, code **76005** for fluoroscopic guidance should be additionally reported. Although not specifically stated in the descriptor nomenclature, injection of contrast material is an inclusive component of codes **64622–64627**, and the contrast should not be reported separately. The Destruction by Neurolytic Agent codes, **64600–64681**, include the injection of other therapeutic agents (eg, corticosteroids).

Eye and Ocular Adnexa

Coding of surgical procedures on the eye and its surrounding tissues can be complex because of the numerous anatomic structures in the ocular system. Therefore, it is important to pay close attention to eye anatomy, each code descriptor, and its location in the Eye and Ocular Adnexa subsection, as well as the appropriate guidelines. The diagnostic and noninvasive tests of the eye are not reported from this section. These are listed in the Medicine section of the CPT codebook, under the Ophthalmology subheading or the appropriate section, such as diagnostic ultrasound. It is also important to note that add-on code **69990**, which describes the use of the operating microscope, is not applicable to any of the codes in the Eye and Ocular Adnexa section. Use of the operating microscope is not reported separately because it is an essential part of many of the procedures described.

The codes in this subsection are divided between the eyeball (the globe) and the ocular adnexa. The codes describing procedures performed on the eyeball include divisions among the globe in its entirety, the anterior segment, and the posterior segment. The further subheadings are anatomically based and then broken into procedure categories.

The ocular adnexa codes are divided anatomically by the extraocular muscles, the eyelids, the conjunctiva, and the orbit. The orbital bones are ordinarily considered part of the musculoskeletal system, but incision and excision of bone(s) of the orbit are described here for convenience of the user of the CPT codebook. Treatments of fractures of the orbital bones are described and coded in the Musculoskeletal System subsection.

A number of codes in the Eye and Ocular Adnexa section contain the phrase "one or more sessions" in their descriptor. When this phrase appears in a code descriptor, the code should be reported only once for the entire defined treatment period, regardless of the number of sessions necessary to complete the treatment. In other words, the code would not be reported for each session in which the patient was seen if it was a visit included in a defined treatment period. The defined treatment period is determined by the physician and varies depending on the patient, diagnosis, and, often, the area to be treated. However, if the patient experiences a recurrence of the condition and retreatment is necessary, then these subsequent retreatment sessions would *not* be considered included in the first treatment series. This retreatment would be reported with the appropriate code, since it represents a new defined treatment period of one or more sessions performed to treat the problem.

Chapter 3

Surgery Exercises

Integumentary System Exercises

EXERCISE 1

If a frozen section pathology report comes back during the same operative session showing that the margins of excision are not adequate, and an additional excision is performed to remove the entire tumor, two codes for excision of lesion should be used.

True or false?

EXERCISE 2

How many codes should be used to report excision of two malignant lesions that fall under the same classification? For example, one lesion is from the left arm with excised diameter of 1.5 cm and one lesion is from the right arm with excised diameter of 2.0 cm.

How is this reported?

A. Report one code. (Add the diameters and choose one code.)
B. Report two codes for each excision.

EXERCISE 3

A patient had a malignant 1.5-cm lesion excised from his leg at a previous operative session. During the postoperative period, a reexcision was necessary because the pathology report showed that the margins were not clear. An additional 0.5 cm from either side of the healing surgical wound was excised, resulting in an excised diameter of 1.0 cm.

The appropriate code(s) to report for the reexcision is:

A. **11601-58**
B. **11601+11602**
C. **11603-58**

EXERCISE 4

How is the appropriate excised diameter determined for reporting the codes for excision of lesions?

A. The measurement of the entire specimen submitted to pathology.
B. The measurement of the lesion itself.
C. The measurement of the greatest clinical diameter of apparent lesion plus the margins required for complete excision.

EXERCISE 5

Special stains are included in code **17304**.

True or false?

EXERCISE 6

Excision of Malignant Lesion and Split-Thickness Graft

A 64-year-old male patient presented with an ill-defined eroded plaque on the dorsal aspect of his hand measuring 1.8-cm in greatest diameter. Biopsy revealed an anaplastic squamous cell carcinoma arising from the epidermis and infiltrating into the deep dermis. In an effort to clear both the clinically apparent and likely inapparent extent of the lesion, a margin of 5 mm (0.5 cm) in width was included in the planned excision. The excised diameter of the lesion was therefore 2.8 cm. The resulting defect could not be closed primarily. A split-thickness skin graft was harvested from the thigh. The graft was then placed over the defect on the hand and sutured in place. At the conclusion of the procedure, a pressure dressing was placed over the surgical sites.

Which code(s) should be reported?

A. **11623** *Excision, malignant lesion including margins, scalp, neck, hands, feet, genitalia; excised diameter 2.1 to 3.0 cm*

B. **11623** *Excision, malignant lesion including margins, scalp, neck, hands, feet, genitalia; excised diameter 2.1 to 3.0 cm*

15120 *Split graft, face, scalp, eyelids, mouth, neck, ears, orbits, genitalia, hands, feet and/or multiple digits; first 100 sq cm or less, or one percent of body area of infants and children (except* **15050***)*

EXERCISE 7

Shaving of Epidural or Dermal Lesions

A 29-year-old patient presented to the dermatologist with a complaint of an enlarging pruritic lesion on her right shoulder. On examination, she was noted to have a 7-mm, fleshy, dome-shaped, nodular lesion with an erythematous base at a site irritated by her bra strap. The impression was of an inflamed nevus.

After discussion of the diagnosis and treatment options with the patient, it was decided to perform a shave removal of the lesion, removing the raised component of the lesion to eliminate future irritation and minimize scarring. The surgical area was prepared, draped, and anesthetized in the usual fashion. The lesion (along with 1-mm margins) was tangentially removed, resulting in a wound that did not extend to fat. Hemostasis was achieved with aluminum chloride, and the wound was dressed with an antibiotic ointment and a dry sterile dressing. Postoperative instructions were reviewed with the patient.

Which code is reported?

A. **11301** *Shaving of epidermal or dermal lesion, single lesion, trunk, arms or legs; lesion diameter 0.6 to 1.0 cm*

B. **11401** *Excision, benign lesion including margins, except skin tag (unless listed elsewhere), trunk, arms or legs; excised diameter 0.6 to 1.0 cm*

EXERCISE 8

Biopsy

A) A suspicious-looking lifelong pigmented mole on a patient's back measuring 0.5 cm was totally excised, along with a margin of 0.2 cm. The excised diameter measured 0.9 cm. The lesion was sent to pathology for evaluation of the lesion and the possible need for further surgery. The lesion was diagnosed as a benign nevus. The correct codes for this service are **11402** and **11100**.

True or false?

B) A basal cell carcinoma on the forehead with an excised diameter of 1.2 cm was excised and the wound was closed in a simple fashion. At the same surgical session, a suspicious lesion on the cheek was noted. A 2-mm punch biopsy of this lesion was also performed. The correct codes for this service are **11642** and **11100-59**.

True or false?

EXERCISE 9

Preoperative Diagnosis: Chronic Paronychia with Recurrent Ingrown Toenail

The affected toe and foot were prepared and draped in the usual sterile fashion. Local anesthesia was administered to the affected toe. A digital tourniquet was used. The affected nail border was freed from soft-tissue attachments by blunt technique using sterile instrumentation. Subungual abscesses were identified and drained. The affected nail was removed with a combination of blunt and sharp dissection. A total matricectomy was performed by surgical excision. Granulomatous tissue was sharply excised and the remaining abscesses were identified and drained. Copious lavage with saline solution was performed. The digital tourniquet was removed, and a mildly compressive dressing with antibiotic cream was applied to the toe.

How is this procedure reported?

EXERCISE 10

History: A patient had a nonhealing ulcer/wound that would benefit from a graft application. The recipient site, because of its presentation and compromised present state, required surgical preparation before graft application.

Preoperative diagnosis: Ulceration (or wound)

Postoperative diagnosis: Same

Procedure: The patient was brought to the procedure room. The area was prepped and draped in the usual sterile manner. Devitalized tissue was debrided free from the surgical site by sharp dissection. The area was then flushed with copious amounts of sterile saline solution. Devitalized tissue was also removed with gentle, mild abrasion of the wound bed to remove loose debris. After healthy viable tissue was exposed and rolled borders were dissected free, the recipient site was once again inspected. Bilaminate skin substitute (less than 25 sq cm) was applied to the recipient site and an appropriate dressing was used.

How is this procedure reported?

Musculoskeletal System Exercises

EXERCISE 1

Preoperative diagnosis: Osteoarthritis and pain in knee

Procedure: Aspiration and Injection of right knee

A 47-year-old female presented with increased pain in the right knee, in which osteoarthritis had been previously diagnosed. Physical examination showed medial joint tenderness, crepitus, and decreased range of motion. A radiograph showed medial joint space narrowing with sclerosis and osteophyte formation. The patient requested a repeat course of hylan G-F 20 (Synvisc) injections, as she had responded well to this treatment 6 months previously. Treatment with several cortisone injections as well as anti-inflammatory medications had failed. Records were reviewed and confirmed the patient's history. There was no history of egg allergy or previous complications, and thus the course of three injections was advised.

Verbal consent was obtained with discussion of unusual risks of bleeding, infection, and possible allergic reaction. Under aseptic conditions, a 22-gauge needle was introduced into the medial joint space, with ethyl chloride spray used for topical anesthesia. No fluid was aspirated, and 2 mL of hylan G-F 20 was injected with no complications. The patient was advised to rest, apply ice, and take 2 acetaminophen tablets (500 mg) if a postinjection flare developed.

How is this procedure reported?

EXERCISE 2

Preoperative diagnosis: Pain and swelling from lateral epicondylitis

Procedure: Injection of tendon origin

A 25-year-old tennis player presented with pain at the left elbow that had developed after a prolonged game 2 weeks earlier. The pain had worsened despite use of over-the-counter ibuprofen and local application of ice. On examination, tenderness was noted at the left lateral epicondyle with worsening of the pain with resisted wrist extension and forced elbow extension. A diagnosis of lateral epicondylitis was made and a cortisone injection was recommended.

Verbal consent was obtained with rare risks of bleeding and infection and tendon rupture discussed Under Aseptic technique, a 22 G needle was introduced into the soft tissue and advanced to the tendon origin with care not to enter the tendon. Ethyl chloride was used for topical anesthesia, and 1%

Lidocaine was injected, as well as 20mg of Depomedrol with immediate improvement in symptoms. Patient was advised to rest and not play tennis for at least a week until symptoms had improved.

How is this procedure reported?

EXERCISE 3

Hammertoe/Bunion Sample Operative Report

Preoperative diagnosis: Hallux abducto valgus left
Hammer toe deformity second left

Postoperative diagnosis: Same

Operations: Bunionectomy with distal, head, or Austin-type osteotomy with internal fixation
Arthroplasty of second toe, left foot

Procedure: The patient was taken to the operating room and placed on the table in the supine position. Monitored anesthesia care with intravenous sedation was then performed. A supramalleolar tourniquet was placed over nonwoven cotton fabric (Webril) padding and inflated to 250 mm Hg for the purpose of hemostasis. The left foot and leg were prepped and draped in the usual sterile fashion. A 50/50 mixture of 1% Lidocaine and 0.5% Marcaine was used about the left forefoot. Attention was directed to the dorsal aspect of the left first metatarsophalangeal joint, where a linear incision was placed just medial to the extensor hallucis longus. The incision was deepened by sharp and blunt dissection down to the level of the capsule, with care taken to maintain adequate surgical hemostasis. The capsule was incised in the standard fashion and dissected from the head of the first metatarsal. Special care was taken to avoid all neurovascular structures. A hypertrophic medial eminence was identified on the first metatarsal and was resected. Attention was directed to the first intermetatarsal space, where the appropriate lateral structures were released.

Attention was redirected medially, where a V-shaped osteotomy was performed.

The capital fragment was shifted laterally into the corrected position and fixated with two 2.7 cortical bone screws or k-wires. At this time, the remaining hypertrophic medial eminence was resected and the wound was flushed copiously with sterile normal saline solution. The capsule was repaired with 3-0 Vicryl, the subcutaneous tissues with 4-0 Vicryl, and the skin margins with a 5-0 Prolene. Attention was directed to the dorsal aspect of the second digit, where a linear incision was placed. The incision was deepened down to the proximal interphalangeal joint capsule, with care taken to maintain adequate surgical hemostasis. The capsule and tendon were sharply incised and dissected from the head of the proximal phalanx. The head of the proximal phalanx was resected in the standard fashion and the wound was flushed copiously with sterile saline. With the digit in the corrected position, the tendon and capsule were repaired with a 4-0 Vicryl and the skin was closed with a 4-0 Prolene. The surgical sites were covered with sterile Adaptec and sterile gauze, and the forefoot was wrapped in a mildly compressive fashion. Deflation of the tourniquet showed immediate and normal return of the vascular status to the entire foot. The patient tolerated the procedures and anesthesia well and left the operating room in stable condition. The patient remained in recovery until stable and was discharged with postoperative instructions and a prescription for an analgesic.

How is this procedure reported?

EXERCISE 4

Preoperative diagnosis: Cervical myelopathy

Postoperative diagnosis: Same

Operations: Anterior cervical diskectomy and foraminotomies at C5-C6 for decompression using microscope and microdissection technique
Anterior cervical arthrodesis at C5-C6
Contouring of allograft
Anterior spinal instrumentation with an anterior cervical plate (C-Tek) at C5-C6

Anesthesia: General

Indications: A 32-year-old female had pain in the back, arm, and neck that was clearly progressing. She had a diskogram that correlated with pain significantly at C5-C6. In view of this finding, an intracervical decompression arthrodesis at C5-C6 was planned.

Procedure: The patient was brought to the operating room on a cart and then transferred to the operating room table in a supine position. General endotracheal anesthesia was administered. The patient's lower extremities were wrapped with Ace wraps. All pressure points were padded. A rolled towel was placed under the patient's posterior cervical area. The patient's arms were placed along the sides with arm boards. A marking incision was made with a No. 10 blade knife in the right anterior cervical area extending just from the midline lateral to the lateral margin of the sternocleidomastoid, two fingerbreadths above the sternal notch. The total length of the excision marked was approximately 8 cm. The area was prepped and draped in the usual sterile manner.

With a No. 15 blade knife, an incision of the right anterior cervical area was made through the skin and subcutaneous tissue to the platysmal fascia. Skin flaps were elevated superiorly and inferiorly with toothed Adson forceps, Metzenbaum scissors, and DeBakey thumb forceps. Angled Weitlaner retractors were placed in the wound.

With the DeBakey thumb forceps and Metzenbaum scissors, the division of the platysmal musculature on the medial border of the right sternocleidomastoid musculature was divided in a muscle-splitting fashion. A plane of dissection was then produced lateral to the trachea and esophagus and medial to the right sternocleidomastoid musculature and carotid sheath to the prevertebral space. A Cloward hand-held retractor was placed in the wound. The C5-C6 interspace was identified and an intraoperative lateral cervical spine x-ray was performed to confirm the location.

A lateral cervical spine x-ray was performed which showed this as being the C5-C6 interspace. Caspar self-retaining retractors were placed in the cervical wound transversely, superiorly, and inferiorly. A standard periosteal dissection was performed on the paired longus colli musculature from the bottom of the vertebral body of C4 to approximately the bottom of the vertebral body of C6 in the midline and extending lateral to the lateral margin of the vertebral bodies of C5-C6. This was done with a No. 15 blade knife and DeBakey thumb forceps with a bunion subperiosteal elevator. A Scoville retractor was then transversely placed deeper in the wound to retract the paired longus colli musculature of the left to the left side and right to the right side. With a No. 15 blade knife, the anterior interspace at C5-C6 was entered.

The intraoperative microscope was brought in, and a standard anterior C5-C6 diskectomy was performed with pituitary biopsy forceps, macrocurets and microcurets, a cutting tool (Midas Rex with AM-35 bit), and 1- and 2-mm Kerrison punches. The vertebral end plates superiorly at C6 and inferiorly at C5 were removed. The posterior longitudinal ligament was entered and resected. The foramina on the right at C5-C6 were enlarged with Kerrison punches and microcurets.

After microscope and microdissection techniques were used, the posterior longitudinal ligament was opened and extended into the left side.

Next, with 1- and 2-mm Kerrison punches, bilateral foraminotomies were performed. The foramina were evaluated with the passing of a nerve hook and were widely patent.

The foramina were enlarged with 1- and 2-mm Kerrison punches. The uncovertebral joint was also thinned with the cutting tool. At this time, the foramina were evaluated with a nerve hook and noted to be widely patent. The cervical wound was irrigated with saline.

Distraction was applied by Kaspar pins in the C5 and C6 vertebral body. An allograft was prepared and then impacted into the interspace at C5-C6 with the use of the Cloward impactor and mallet. Bone graft material was noted to be fitted appropriately, and the posterior portion of the bone graft material was noted to be well away from the dura.

Using a C-Tek MRI (magnetic resonance imaging)–compatible anterior cervical plate was contoured to fit the anterior vertebral body at C5-C6. The plate was secured at all four locations with MRI-compatible self-tapping screws. The screw holes were made with a pilot drill and appropriate drill guide. The holes were tapped with an appropriate-sized tap, and the screws were placed and sequentially tightened with a hexagonal wrench. After the screws were tightened, the locking screws on the plate were tightened with a torque wrench. All of the retractors were removed from the wound. The wound was irrigated with saline.

A lateral cervical spine x-ray was performed. This demonstrated appropriate placement of the anterior interbody fusion and segmental spinal instrumentation at C5-C6.

The cervical wound was irrigated with saline. The paired longus colli muscles were reapproximated at the midline with a figure-of-eight suture of 3-0 Vicryl. The platysmal musculature was then closed in a separate layer with interrupted figure-of-eight suture of 3-0 Vicryl and subcutaneous tissue was closed with interrupted 3-0 Vicryl suture. The skin was then closed with a running intracuticular suture of 4-0 Vicryl. The wound was washed and dried, and half-inch adhesive strips were applied. A surgical dressing sponge (Telfa) was placed. The drapes were removed. The dressing was secured to the skin with three-inch paper tape. The posterior cervical roll was removed. A cervical collar was applied. The patient tolerated the procedure without difficulty.

How is this procedure reported?

EXERCISE 5

A 30-year-old male presented to the emergency department after falling off of a ladder. The emergency department physician determined that the patient's left forearm was fractured. The physician then applied a short arm cast and instructed the patient to follow up with an orthopedic physician.

How would the emergency department physician's services be coded?

EXERCISE 6

A 10-year-old male presented to the emergency department after falling and fracturing his tibia. The emergency department physician called an orthopedic surgeon for a consultation. The orthopedic physician evaluated the patient, performed a closed reduction of the tibia, and applied a long leg cast.

How would the services for the emergency department physician and/or orthopedic surgeon be coded?

EXERCISE 7

History: This is a male patient who has had left shoulder pain since April 2000 when he attempted to lift a utility underground vault manhole lid at work. He was previously treated with physical therapy and anti-inflammatory medications, but has failed to see improvement. A magnetic resonance imaging (MRI) showed posttraumatic degenerative changes of the acromioclavicular joint with some tearing of the superior labrum.

Preoperative diagnosis: Left shoulder impingement syndrome with possible partial rotator cuff tear

Postoperative diagnosis: Same; with torn, frayed anterior superior glenoid labrum and fraying of the undersurface of the rotator cuff

Operations: Diagnostic and surgical arthroscopy of the left shoulder
Arthroscopic limited debridement of the anterior superior labrum and the undersurface of the supraspinatus tendon of the left shoulder
Arthroscopic acromioplasty and arch decompression of the left shoulder
Resection of the coracoacromial ligament

Diagnostic findings: Diagnostic arthroscopy showed a torn, frayed anterior superior glenoid labrum. There was partial fraying and degenerative tearing of the undersurface of the supraspinatus tendon. Subacromial bursoscopy showed thickening of the subacromial bursal tissue with an anterior inferior subacromial spur.

Procedure: The patient was brought to the operating room and placed in a supine position on the operating table. General anesthesia was given successfully via endotracheal intubation. The patient was placed in the sitting position in the beach-chair position. The upper extremity was then prepared and draped in the usual sterile fashion.

A stab incision was made in the posterior aspect of the shoulder with a No. 11 blade. With inflow occurring in the pump, a Stryker arthroscope was bluntly introduced through the posterior portal into the glenohumeral joint space. Inspection of the joint space began at the biceps tendon, which showed no significant fraying or inflammation. The undersurface of the rotator cuff was then inspected, and there was no evidence of rotator cuff tearing or fraying. The undersurface of the supraspinatus tendon showed partial fraying and degenerative tearing. The infraspinatus and teres minor portions of the rotator cuff were intact. The posterior aspect of the humeral head was normal, with no significant chondromalacia. The inferior recess showed no evidence of loose bodies. The posterior labrum showed no evidence of tearing. There was a torn frayed anterior superior labrum.

Through an anterior superior portal, the frayed and torn labral tissues and the frayed and torn rotator cuff tissues were excised and debrided. The anterior inferior glenohumeral ligament and the anterior middle glenoid ligament were normal and well attached to the glenoid. The arthroscope was then removed from the glenohumeral joint space.

Through a posterolateral portal, the arthroscope was placed into the subacromial bursal space with inflow cannula established through the arthroscope. The subacromial bursal space showed thickening of the subacromial bursal tissue. A full-radius shaver was brought in through an anterolateral portal and the bursal tissue was removed. There was scuffing and fraying of the coracoacromial ligament. The anterior inferior acromion had an anterior inferior subacromial spur. With a combination of burs and shavers, an anterior inferior acromioplasty was performed by removing the anterior inferior portion of the undersurface of the acromion. The superior surface of the rotator cuff was then inspected and no rotator cuff tears were found.

The instruments were then removed from the shoulder. The portal sites were closed with 3-0 Vicryl. Adhesive strips, sterile dressings, and a sling were applied. The patient was then placed in the supine position, awakened successfully, and sent to the recovery room in stable condition. There were no operative complications. Sponge, needle, and instrument counts were reported correctly at the conclusion of the procedure.

How is this procedure reported?

EXERCISE 8

History: A 21-year-old skier tore the posterior cruciate ligament, requiring arthroscopically aided ligament reconstruction

Procedure: A bone-middle third patella tendon-bone autograft was harvested through an anterior incision by means of an oscillating saw to remove bone plugs and contiguous middle third patella tendon.

After graft preparation was complete, the arthroscopic instruments were inserted into the knee with gravity or pump inflow through a superior arthroscopic portal. The arthroscope was inserted from an inferior lateral portal. Instrumentation for the procedure was brought in through an inferior medial patella portal. Video arthroscopy of the procedure with appropriate photographs and videotaping was frequently done. A 2-cm incision was made into the posterior medial skin, allowing protection of the posterior neurovascular structures and permitting the surgeon to monitor the instruments passed from the front to the back of the knee joint. This posterior medial incision began at the level of the knee joint and extended distally approximately 2 cm. After opening of the deep fascia, the surgeon's finger was passed anteriorly to the medial head of the gastrocnemius muscle and neurovascular structures and posteriorly to the capsule of the knee joint. The posterior cruciate ligament fossa was palpated through the capsule. Intraoperative x-ray (C-arm fluoroscopy) was used periodically during the procedure to ensure proper placement of drill guides and drills, and to ensure the safety of the posterior neurovascular structures.

A "notch plasty" was performed to enlarge the intercondylar notch with a power burr. The posterior cruciate ligament stumps were debrided with a power instrument, leaving remnants to serve as anatomic landmarks. The posterior cruciate ligament fossa was debrided and the posterior capsule was elevated from bone with a special curved knife, rasp, and elevator. The surgeon's finger was placed posteromedially to ensure that this latter dissection was done safely and in its proper location. This capsular elevation extended approximately 2 cm below the posterior tibial ridge.

A drill guide was positioned so that the guide wire entered the anterior medial proximal tibia approximately 2 cm below the tibial tubercle and exited the tibial ridge posteriorly. The tip of the guide wire was monitored at all times by the fluoroscopic C-arm. The tibial tunnel was made with a cannulated tibial reamer, using the fluoroscopic C-arm to prevent the reamer from overpenetrating the posterior aspect of the tibia. Soft tissue was carefully removed from the openings of the tunnel. The femoral tunnels were made by passing guide wires from outside the knee with a drill guide to enter the knee joint at points along the lateral wall of the medial femoral condyle, which approached isometric graft placement. The femoral tunnels were reamed to the same size as the graft material. All reaming debris was evacuated with motorized instrumentation. A wire was passed through the tibial tunnel into the back of the knee joint. The wire was then pulled out through the femoral tunnel. (This was a very difficult and time-consuming portion of the procedure, since the wire must pass sharply at the posterior aspect of the tibial tunnel at the rear of the knee and then around into the center of the knee joint, where it must then be grasped with arthroscopic tools and pulled up into the femoral tunnel.) A flexible rasp was then attached to the wire and pulled through both tunnels to smooth the tissues around the tunnel edges. The graft material was attached to the end of the flexible rasp with traction sutures and then pulled into position. The graft material was then secured at the tibial tunnel and the femoral tunnels with interference screw or button and suture fixation. Care was taken before the graft was secured so that no impingement on the graft occurred from the surrounding bone during the full range of motion. Further, there was no bony impingement on the graft in the intercondylar notch. The knee was tested for proper ligament stability by adjusting the positioning of the graft. An interarticular drain was placed and brought out through the skin at one of the arthroscopic portals. The posterior medial skin incision was closed in layers.

How is this procedure reported?

Respiratory System Exercises

EXERCISE 1

History: A 68-year-old female had peripheral alveolar infiltrates in the right lower lobes that had been unchanged for 6 weeks.

Procedure: Once the patient was properly sedated and locally anesthetized, the oxygen was turned up to 5 L/min. A fiberoptic bronchoscope was inserted through the nostril, visualizing the upper airways to the vocal cords. The vocal cords were visualized and observed for function. The bronchoscope was advanced into the trachea and all of the airways were inspected. Forceps were advanced through the suction channel of the bronchoscope into the right lower-lobe bronchus, leading to the infiltrate. A fluoroscope was activated and the biopsy forceps were advanced into the infiltrate, then backed off by 1 to 2 cm. Under fluoroscopic guidance, the forceps were opened, a transbronchial biopsy was obtained on expiration, and the forceps were removed. Three to six biopsies were obtained in one lobe with fluoroscopic guidance. The bronchoscope was withdrawn from the airways, carefully visualizing the trachea, and then withdrawn from the patient. The chest was inspected for a pneumothorax with the fluoroscope. The biopsies were placed in formalin and sent to Pathology.

How is this procedure reported?

EXERCISE 2

Preoperative diagnosis: Deviated nasal septum with nasal deformity, chronic sinusitis

Postoperative diagnosis: Same

Operations: Submucous resection and nasal reconstruction
Limited endoscopic sinus surgery

Anesthesia: Intravenous sedation

Procedure: With the patient in the supine position under intravenous sedation, prepping and draping were done in the usual manner. Cocaine, 4%, was applied topically with cottonoids, and Xylocaine, 1% with epinephrine, was infiltrated in the area of the nasal septum as well as the nasal dorsum. Intercartilaginous incisions were then made on either side of the upper lateral cartilage area, and the upper lateral cartilages were then separated from the nasal skin. Nasal bone periosteum was then elevated with the help of a Joseph knife and Joseph elevator. The incisions on either side were connected in the midline with Metzenbaum scissors and the nasal dorsal hump was completely uncovered. An incision was brought over the caudal portion of the septum with a button hand knife, and a complete transfixion incision was made. The mucoperichondrium over the nasal septum was then elevated and the deviated portion of the septum was identified. This was found to be on the left side, with a large spur blocking the nasal passages. A strip of cartilage measuring approximately 2 mm was then removed from the anterior portion of the nasal septum in the caudal portion. After elevation of the mucoperiosteum and perichondrium, a strut of cartilage measuring approximately 1.5 cm was left anteriorly in place. The posterior portion of the septum, which was deviated, was removed partially with a Ballenger knife as well as with Takahashi forceps. The spur was then elevated off of the mucoperiosteum and removed with a bone rongeur and chisel. A perpendicular plate of the ethmoid was found to be causing a severe deviation in the posterior portion, which was also elevated off the mucoperiosteum, and the bone was removed in bits and pieces with Takahashi forceps. The septum was then placed toward the midline. At this point, upper lateral cartilage was separated from the nasal septum and lower lateral cartilages were trimmed with the help of a rim incision. An excess portion of the upper lateral cartilage was trimmed with upper lateral scissors. The nasal dorsal hump was then removed with a No. 11 blade in the cartilaginous portion and Rubin osteotome in the bony portion. Medial osteotomies were performed. Incisions were closed with 3-0 chromic catgut for complete transfixion incision and 4-0 chromic for the others. Lateral osteotomies were done in a curvilinear fashion. Nasal packing was then placed into the nasal cavity. The nose was taped and a Denver splint was applied.

Upon completion of the submucous resection nasal reconstruction, a 30° endoscope was used to visualize the nasal cavity and check the turbinates as well as the septum. The area of the middle turbinates on either side was found to be hypertrophic, and in this area the maxillary sinus ostium was stenotic. The uncinate process was then elevated and partial ethmoidectomy was carried out by using Kennedy forceps, and the maxillary sinus ostium was widened with backbiting forceps. The same procedure was then repeated on the opposite side, with similar findings. The middle turbinate on the right side was then partially resected and the maxillary sinus ostium was widened.

The procedure was then terminated. Nasal packing was applied. Vaseline gauze soaked in bacitracin, as well as nasal dressings, were applied. The patient was then returned to recovery in good condition. Bleeding was minimal.

How is this procedure reported?

Cardiovascular System Exercises

EXERCISE 1

Removal of an existing pacing cardioverter-defibrillator device is not included in the replacement code and should be separately reported.

True or false?

EXERCISE 2

How is replacement of a dual-chamber permanent pacemaker and transvenous electrodes with a new dual-chamber permanent pacemaker and electrodes reported?

EXERCISE 3

Harvesting of the radial artery for coronary artery bypass procedure is reported with which code(s)?

EXERCISE 4

The procurement of an upper-extremity vein is included when a coronary artery or lower-extremity bypass procedure is reported.

True or false?

EXERCISE 5

A redo coronary artery bypass graft was performed on a patient involving the left internal mammary artery to the left anterior descending artery and a saphenous vein graft to the right coronary artery. The original coronary artery bypass grafting was performed 2 years earlier.

How is this procedure reported?

Digestive System Exercises

EXERCISE 1

Colonoscopy With Removal of Polyp With Cold Biopsy Forceps

Indications: Colorectal cancer screening, high risk with family history of colon cancer

Procedure: After informed consent was obtained, the patient was sedated with Demerol 50 mg and Versed 2 mg. Full monitoring with pulse oximetry, electrocardiography, and blood pressure monitoring was performed. With the patient in the left lateral decubitus position, the adult colonoscope was inserted after digital examination showed the rectum to be normal.

Retroversion of the endoscope in the rectum showed no abnormalities, and the sigmoid appeared normal. The descending colon, transverse colon, ascending colon, and ileocecal valve were normal. However, in the hepatic flexure area, a 3-mm polyp was seen and documented photographically. It was completely removed with the cold biopsy forceps. The patient was then turned onto his back for withdrawal of the colonoscope and to afford a different view of the colon on removal of the instrument. No other abnormalities were found.

How is this procedure reported?

EXERCISE 2

Screening Colonoscopy Converted to Colonoscopy With Polypectomy

Indications: Colorectal cancer screening in an average-risk, 73-year-old male with no gastrointestinal complaints

Procedure: Informed consent was obtained and intravenous sedation was given with 50 mg of Demerol and 3 mg of Versed to the point of light sedation. Full cardiac, blood pressure, and pulse oximetry monitoring was carried out. With the patient in the left lateral decubitus position, the video colonoscope was introduced into the rectum, and retroflexion showed small internal hemorrhoids. In the midsigmoid there was moderate diverticulosis without inflammation. In the transverse colon, a 1.5-cm, benign-appearing pedunculated polyp was seen and documented photographically. It was removed by snare polypectomy with cautery and retrieved for pathology. The scope was then inserted into the remainder of the colon, and the cecum and ileocecal valve were reached. Preparation was excellent. The patient was then turned onto his back to provide a different view on withdrawal of the colonoscope, and no other abnormalities were found. He tolerated the procedure well and was returned to recovery in stable condition.

How is this procedure reported?

> **CODING TIP**
>
> Because the coding guidelines in the CPT codebook state that a surgical endoscopy always includes a diagnostic endoscopy, the diagnostic colonoscopy is included in the surgical colonoscopy.

EXERCISE 3

Unusual Procedure or Service

Indications: Surveillance for dysplasia in a patient with a 14-year history of ulcerative colitis with documentation of complete colon involvement in the past

> **CODING TIP**
>
> Complications, exacerbations, recurrence, or the presence of other diseases or injuries requiring additional services should be reported separately.

Procedure: Informed consent was obtained. The patient was given 50 mg of Demerol and 3 mg of Versed intravenously and was monitored by blood pressure, electrocardiography, and pulse oximetry. The video colonoscope was inserted in the rectum and advanced under direct vision through the rectosigmoid after retroversion had been carried out. The rectosigmoid had a significant amount of friability and microerosions compatible with mildly active ulcerative colitis. The mucosal markings appeared more normal above 50 cm, and the remainder of the descending colon and transverse, ascending, and cecal areas appeared somewhat atrophic but otherwise normal. The cecal pole was reached and the ileocecal valve was intubated. The terminal ileum appeared somewhat dilated and was compatible with backwash ileitis.

The scope was then slowly withdrawn from the cecum, with four biopsy specimens being taken from the four different quadrants every 10 cm. A total of 48 biopsies were taken and placed in four separate bottles denoting their location in the colon. No abnormalities were seen other than those described above. The patient tolerated the procedure well and was returned to his room in stable condition. Because of the multiplicity of biopsies, this procedure took three times as long as the average standard colonoscopy with biopsies.

How is this procedure reported?

> **CODING TIP**
>
> Medicare has specific policy for the billing and reimbursement of multiple procedures performed during the same endoscopy. However, reporting requirements may differ with each carrier. The third-party payer's specific reporting requirements should be determined.

EXERCISE 4

Multiple Procedures During the Same Endoscopy

Indications: History of nausea and vomiting after gastric bypass surgery, with abnormal upper gastrointestinal series suggestive of either ulceration or early fistula formation

Procedure: After informed consent was obtained and the patient was sedated with 50 mg of Demerol and 3 mg of Versed, the endoscope was introduced under direct visualization and advanced to the small bowel. The esophagus was normal. Upon entering the stomach, postsurgical changes were seen.

The suture line was clearly visible on retroflexed examination and appeared to be intact. There appeared to be some shallow erosions that were in the healing stage and the mucosa was friable, but no active bleeding was seen. Biopsies were performed. No other abnormalities were seen. The gastrojejunal anastomosis was slightly tight, and with some mild difficulty the endoscope could be pushed through the anastomosis. The luminal diameter of the anastomosis was approximately 8 mm. Just below the gastrojejunal anastomosis, in the small bowel, there appeared to be an offshoot of bowel, immediately distal to the anastomosis. This was intubated and appeared to be a blind loop, but no evidence of friability or fistula formation was seen. The endoscope was then pulled back to the anastomosis and pushed forward into the other loop, where the jejunum itself could be visualized. The endoscope was advanced into the jejunum; no stricture formation was seen.

The endoscope was withdrawn into the stomach. A "through the scope" balloon was advanced through the endoscope and positioned across the anastomosis. Balloon dilation of the anastomosis was performed to 12 mm and then increased to 13.5 mm under direct visualization. No bleeding was seen. The endoscope was then withdrawn. The patient tolerated the procedure well. Postprocedure vital signs were stable, and the patient went to the recovery suite for observation.

How is this procedure reported?

EXERCISE 5

Multiple Procedures Performed During the Same Endoscopy

Indications: Jaundice, weight loss, abnormal computed tomography scan

Procedure: Informed consent was obtained. The patient received a total of 100 mg of Demerol and 3 mg of Versed intravenously during the procedure. Examination of the esophagus, stomach, and duodenal bulb was unremarkable. The major papilla was normal in appearance. A cholangiogram and pancreatogram were obtained with a sphincterotome. A narrowed, strictured area was identified in the proximal bile duct. A guide wire was advanced into the proximal bile duct and a medium-sized sphincterotomy was done without apparent complications. At this point, the sphincterotome was exchanged for a cytobrush, and brushings were obtained from the bile duct stricture. After this, the cytobrush was removed and a 10 French/5 cm straight stent was advanced over the guide wire by means of the standard pushing device. This was placed in good position across the stricture, with free flow of bile noted after placement. The endoscope was then withdrawn. The procedure lasted approximately 1 hour and was well tolerated. The patient was returned to the recovery suite; postprocedure vital signs were stable.

How is this procedure reported?

CODING TIP

From a CPT coding perspective, if a provider performs multiple procedures on the same date of service, there are certain guidelines within the CPT coding system that indicate how the procedures should be reported. When multiple procedures, other than E/M services, are performed on the same day or at the same session by the same provider, the major primary procedure or service may be reported as listed. The secondary additional or lesser procedure(s) or service(s) may be identified by appending modifier 51, Multiple Procedures, to the secondary additional procedure or service code(s). This modifier may be used to report multiple medical procedures performed at the same session, as well as a combination of medical and surgical procedures, or several surgical procedures performed at the same operative session.

CODING TIP

If the biopsies were so extensive as to require significantly more time than an average procedure, modifier 22 can be appended, as illustrated in Exercise 3. The claim must be submitted with the procedure report as well as a short statement indicating the complexity of the procedure and the additional time it took to perform. Modifier 22 should be used only when the expectation of increased reimbursement is significant, as the claim will require manual review and may take several months for processing.

EXERCISE 6

Indications: Chronic diarrhea and blood in stool in a patient who had undergone subtotal colectomy for neoplasm

Medications: Conscious sedation to insure adequate patient safety and comfort

Procedure: Informed consent was obtained. The patient received a total of 50 mg of meperidine and 5 mg of midazolam hydrochloride in an intravenous push given in slow incremental doses with continuous monitoring throughout the procedure to achieve conscious sedation. The patient was placed in the left lateral decubitus position. The video colonoscope was introduced. The instrument was advanced to the level of the ileocolic anastomosis and into the distal portion of the terminal ileum. The ileocolic anastomosis was seen at 25 cm. The instrument was advanced to a total depth of approximately 38 cm. The examination of the terminal ileum was remarkable for some mild mucosal erythema. No ulcerations or erosions were seen. Multiple biopsies were performed. The ileocolic anastomosis was seen at 25 cm. This was also remarkable for some mild mucosal erythema and biopsies were obtained. The examination of the distal 25 cm of remaining colon again showed mild mucosal erythema and edema with some obscuring of the mucosal vascular markings. No ulcerations were noted. No neoplastic change was seen. Biopsy specimens were obtained at 18 cm and from the distal rectum. Retroflexion view of the rectum on withdrawal showed no other changes.

How is this procedure reported?

Urinary System Exercises

EXERCISE 1

History: A 67-year-old male presented with bilateral urolithiasis, with stones measuring 3.0 cm on the right and 1.8 cm on the left. One month later, the patient was experiencing severe right flank pain for which there had been no relief. Extracorporeal shock-wave lithotripsy was performed on the right stone only. It was explained to the patient that if the lithotripsy was not sufficient to fragment the stone into pieces small enough to enable passage down the ureter, further treatment might be necessary.

Procedure: After consent was obtained, the patient was taken to the operating room, where he was placed on the gurney. The stone was localized by a combination of ultrasound and fluoroscopy, and the ultrasound machine was positioned. Monitored anesthesia care was achieved, after which the patient received 2500 shocks of power levels graded from 1 up to 6, with good fragmentation of the stone. A double-J stent was inserted in the right ureter to enable passage of the stone fragments and was planned to be removed the next day. Once this was done, the patient was aroused and taken off the table for discharge into the recovery room.

How is this procedure reported?

EXERCISE 2

This procedure is a continuation of Exercise 1 with the same patient.

History: A 67-year-old male had had a 3.0-cm stone in his right renal pelvis, which had been treated with extracorporeal shock-wave lithotripsy 30 days previously, and a 1.8-cm stone in his left renal pelvis. Approximately three days previously, the patient had presented with severe right renal colic, which was refractory to pain meds and a rising white blood cell count to 20. He was admitted to the hospital. A computed tomographic scan showed a large amount of stone fragments, approximately 5 cm long, in the ureter on the right side. There was also a 1.5-cm renal pelvic fragment remaining on the right side. On the left side, he had a renal pelvis stone, as described before, of 1.8 cm with partial obstruction. After explaining all risks and benefits, the urologist elected to treat the stones in both upper tracts.

Procedure: After consent was obtained, the patient was taken to the operating room, where he was prepped and draped in the standard sterile dorsolithotomy position after induction of general anesthesia. With fluoroscopic guidance, a cystoscope was passed through the urethra, the bladder was drained, and a guide wire was passed after much difficulty through the right ureteral stone fragments. Once the guide wire was in place, a rigid ureteroscope was passed up the ureter, where multiple stones of 3 to 4 mm in caliber were found. All of the ureteral stones were broken up with a homium laser and 400 Micron laser fiber until fragments less than 1 to 2 mm were produced. A stone cup was passed beyond them, and they were evacuated out of the kidney. With the guide wire still in place, the flexible ureteroscope was then passed over the guide wire and into the renal pelvis. In the midpole, a 1.5-cm stone was broken up into 1- to 2-mm fragments with a 400 Micron laser fiber. The guide was then replaced, and a 26-cm, 7 French JJ stent was placed. This was noted to be in correct position by fluoroscopy and direct vision.

At this point, attention was turned to the left ureteral orifice. A guide wire was passed into the left renal pelvis. A flexible ureteroscope was then passed over it and all the calyces were examined. The 1.8-cm stone could not be seen; at this point, a retrograde pyelogram was performed and showed the stone to be in a lower-pole calyx. The stone was broken up with a 200 Micron fiber into 2- and 3-mm fragments. The stones were then flushed out of the bladder with sterile saline solution. A 26-cm, 7F JJ stent was then placed and was noted to be curled up in the renal pelvic and the bladder. The bladder was then emptied. The patient was aroused and discharged to the recovery room.

How is this procedure reported?

EXERCISE 3

A 70-year-old male had severe obstructive symptoms secondary to benign prostatic hyperplasia/hypertrophy. During cystoscopic examination under anesthesia, a 25-gram obstructive prostate was noted. A right-angle Nd:YAG laser fiber was passed into the prostatic fossa through a continuous-flow resectoscope, and 60 W of laser energy was delivered for 90 seconds in each of four quadrants and to the median lobe. The procedure was 45 minutes in duration. The patient had a catheter placed and was discharged the next day on drainage. He returned to the office on the fifth postoperative day, and his Foley catheter was removed. He was treated with intermittent catheterization until he began to void well, by the second postoperative week.

How is this procedure reported?

EXERCISE 4

A 75-year-old male had severe obstructive symptoms secondary to benign prostatic hyperplasia/hypertrophy. During cystoscopic examination under anesthesia, a 65-g obstructive prostate was noted. A right-angle Nd:YAG laser fiber was passed into the prostatic fossa through a continuous-flow resectoscope with the use of 80 W of laser energy for 45 seconds at a time. Prostate tissue was vaporized at 20 different points within the prostatic fossa, ultimately creating a resected cavity similar to that obtained with transurethral resection of the prostate. The procedure was one hour in duration. A catheter was placed and the patient was discharged on the second postoperative day. He returned to the office on the fifth postoperative day and his Foley catheter was removed with a voiding trial.

How is this procedure reported?

Female Genital System Exercises

EXERCISE 1

A 28-year-old patient was seen by her family physician for a well-woman examination. The Papanicolau smear report indicated an abnormality. The family physician requested that the patient be seen in consultation by a gynecologist. The family physician wrote the gynecologist that, in addition to the abnormal Papanicolau smear, the patient had a one-year history of vulvar irritation and itching that had been unresponsive to antifungal and antibiotic cream preparations. The gynecologist subsequently saw the patient, reviewed the intake history, and discussed the year-long complaint and treatment of the vulvar irritation. The patient reported that the itching had persisted for more than a year. It was not related to her menstrual cycle. The creams were of little help, as the patient experienced a sensation of mild burning irritation all the time. Her vital signs included blood pressure of 124/82 mm Hg, height of 5ft 7 in, and weight of 156 lb. Her orientation, mental status, and appearance were normal.

After discussing the Papanicolau smear report and receiving informed consent, the gynecologist performed vulvar and cervical colposcopies. Suspicious lesions were noted on the vulva and just inside the endocervical canal. A biopsy specimen of the vulvar lesion was obtained and an endocervical curettage was performed. The gynecologist sent a letter back to the family physician describing the findings and the proposed treatment plan.

How is this procedure reported?

EXERCISE 2

History: A 32-year-old female was diagnosed with infertility caused by adhesions of both fallopian tubes. After a discussion of the risks, the physician scheduled a fimbrioplasty.

Preoperative diagnosis: Infertility caused by adhesions

Postoperative diagnosis: Same

Operation: Bilateral fimbrioplasty

Procedure: Through an incision just above the pubic hairline, the existing fimbriae were reconstructed in the obstructed oviducts. The fimbrial adhesions on the left and right were lysed and material was applied to prevent future adhesions. After the procedure, a chromotubation was performed to ensure that the tubes were patent.

How is this procedure reported?

EXERCISE 3

Preoperative diagnosis: Endometriosis of uterus; vaginal enterocele

Postoperative diagnosis: Same

Operations: Supracervical abdominal hysterectomy; repair of enterocele

Procedure: A horizontal incision within the pubic hairline was made. The uterus and left ovary and fallopian tube were removed. The supporting pedicles containing the tubes, ligaments, and arteries were clamped and cut free. The uterus was cut free from the cervix, leaving the cervix still attached to the vagina. The abdominal incision was then closed with sutures. Through the vagina, the enterocele sac was incised and ligated and the uterosacral ligaments and endopelvic fascia were approximated anterior to the rectum. The vaginal epithelium was then closed.

How is this procedure reported?

EXERCISE 4

A diagnostic laparoscopy was performed on a patient with genuine stress urinary incontinence. During the diagnostic laparoscopy, multiple small submucosal fibroids were noted. A laparoscopic vaginal hysterectomy and a laparoscopic Burch procedure were performed during the same surgical session on the patient. The pathology report indicated that the uterus weighed 230 grams and that there were seven fibroid tumors ranging in size from 0.8 cm to 3.5 cm.

How is this procedure reported?

EXERCISE 5

Preoperative diagnosis: Endometriosis of fallopian tube; uterine polyp

Postoperative diagnosis: Same

Operation: Laparoscopic removal of endometrial implants; polypectomy

A 28-year-old patient underwent a laparoscopy for pelvic pain and a hysteroscopy for abnormal uterine bleeding. The preoperative diagnoses were endometriosis of the fallopian tube and uterine polyp. During the laparoscopy, multiple endometriotic implants were identified and cautery was used to destroy them. During the hysteroscopy, a polyp was identified and a dilation and curettage and polypectomy were performed.

How is this procedure reported?

Maternity Care and Delivery Exercises

EXERCISE 1

A 27-year-old, gravida 1, para 0 patient had been managed in the antepartum period by her family physician, who saw her for 12 visits. At 40 weeks, 3 days, she was admitted to the hospital in active labor at 10 AM. She progressed well with artificial rupture of the membranes, and an epidural catheter was placed when her cervix was 5 cm dilated. Fetal heart tones remained normal. The cervix was completely dilated and 0 station at 5 PM. However, after one and one-half hours of pushing, the vertex was firmly wedged in the pelvis at 0 station. The family physician requested a consultation from an obstetrician. The obstetrician reviewed the patient's prenatal history, assessed her mental status, performed an abdominal examination, listened to her heart and lungs, palpated the fetus abdominally, and performed a pelvic examination to assess the bony pelvis, cervix, and presenting vertex of the fetus. The obstetrician then discussed the situation with the patient and her husband and recommended a cesarean delivery. This discussion took 20 minutes, during which time informed consent was obtained. The patient was taken to the operating room for a cesarean delivery by the obstetrician at 7:15 PM. The obstetrician provided her hospital care and 6-week postpartum office care.

How is this procedure reported?

Nervous System Exercises

EXERCISE 1

When stereotactic radiosurgery is performed with a gamma knife, can code **61793** *be reported twice if the patient has two lesions being treated, one on the right side and one on the left? How is this procedure reported?*

EXERCISE 2

If destruction by a neurolytic agent of the paravertebral facet joint on both left and right sides at the L5 level is performed, then code **64622** is reported only once for the L5 level.

True or false?

EXERCISE 3

A 27-year-old female patient was receiving the dopamine-receptor blocking agent pimozide for treatment of Tourette syndrome. She developed tardive dystonia with severe arching of her back. The patient was unresponsive to and had side effects from oral medications. Through clinical examination and available electrodiagnostic information, the erector spinae muscles were identified. The sites were prepped and localized. Injections of botulinum toxin were administered to multiple sites along the muscle. Several muscles were injected. A report was dictated.

How is this procedure reported?

Eye and Ocular Adnexa Exercises

EXERCISE 1

Preoperative diagnosis: Glaucoma, no history of previous surgical intervention

Postoperative diagnosis: Same

Operation: Trabeculectomy, left eye

Procedure: After administration of retrobulbar local anesthesia, the operating microscope was positioned, the globe was rotated inferiorly, and a stay suture was placed in the superior rectus muscle to permit good surgical exposure during the procedure. A curved incision was made in the conjunctiva near the fornix (the fold of conjunctiva at the junction of the eyelid and the sclera), so that the base or bottom of the conjunctival flap was located at the limbus. Connective tissue beneath the conjunctiva was dissected to expose the sclera. Dissection continued down to the surgical limbus. The conjunctiva, which would subsequently be used to form a flap or bleb to function as a reservoir for aqueous, was folded downward over the cornea to expose the sclera.

A three-sided rectangular or two-sided triangular scleral flap was created by incising the sclera, forming a lamellar flap from one-third to one-half its thickness. An antifibrotic agent was applied after creation of the scleral flap. A sponge soaked with the antifibrotic agent and balanced saline solution was placed on the scleral flap for 5 minutes and then removed. A self-sealing stab wound paracentesis (not coded separately) was performed at another site to be available for introduction of viscoelastic agent or for reforming the anterior chamber at the conclusion of the procedure.

Next, the scleral flap was raised and a small incision was made into the anterior chamber beneath the base of the scleral flap. A small block of trabecular mesh tissue was removed to create an opening (fistula) to allow aqueous to flow out of the anterior chamber. A peripheral iridectomy (not coded separately) was performed next as a routine component of trabeculectomy to promote flow of aqueous from the posterior chamber to the anterior chamber (and also to keep the iris from plugging the drainage path). The scleral flap was closed with releasable sutures. The conjunctival flap was placed over the scleral flap and sutured with a watertight closure. This step formed a bleb or reservoir to hold aqueous fluid that flowed out of the anterior chamber, through the fistula, and beneath the scleral flap to reach the subconjunctival space, where it was absorbed naturally by the body. Next, balanced saline solution was injected into the anterior chamber to reform it. Once it was reformed, the flow of aqueous was checked for the desired slow flow through the scleral flap. The watertight seal of the bleb was also checked to be certain there were no leaks. During the postoperative period, releasable sutures were removed one at a time, on the basis of the adequacy of the bleb's function. Suture removal was included and was not reported separately by the physician.

How is this procedure reported?

EXERCISE 2

A patient visited his ophthalmologist because of problems with the retina in his left eye. The ophthalmologist recommended laser photocoagulation treatment(s) for prophylaxis of retinal detachment and documented this in the record. In the outpatient setting, the patient underwent laser photocoagulation on April 1, April 15, and May 15.

How are these treatments coded?

A. **67145**; **67145-51**; **67145-51** *Reported three times for each date and modifier 51 appended to indicate multiple procedures*

B. **67145** *Reported once for all dates*

C. **67145**; **67145-59**; **67145-59** *Reported three times for each date and modifier 59 appended to indicate separate procedures*

EXERCISE 3

Preoperative diagnosis: Senile cataract, right eye
Diabetic retinopathy, both eyes
Status post vitrectomy, right eye
Status post retinal laser, both eyes

Postoperative diagnosis: Senile cataract, right eye
Diabetic retinopathy, both eyes
Status postvitrectomy, right eye
Status postretinal laser, both eyes

Operations: Cataract extraction and intraocular lens implant insertion, right eye

Anesthesia: Local, standby

Complications: Dislocated cataract, right eye

Procedure: The patient and the eye to be operated on were identified in the operating room. The patient received a retrobulbar block anesthetic in the right eye. The eye was again prepared and the patient was draped in a routine manner. Jaffe blepharostats were inserted between the upper and lower lids. A superior rectus fixation suture was applied. A peritomy was performed superiorly. Episcleral vessels were cauterized. A posterior limbal scratch incision 3 mm in length was made. A tunnel was dissected anteriorly into clear cornea. A paracentesis tract was placed at the two o'clock position. The anterior chamber was entered with a 2.85-mm keratome blade. Hyaluronate sodium (Healon) was used to inflate the anterior chamber. A 4-mm capsulorrhexis was performed. Hydrodissection was attempted with balanced saline solution. It was immediately recognized that the anterior chamber was deepened at the six o'clock position. The lens posterior capsule was thought to have ruptured. The phacoemulsification handpiece needle was embedded in the lens in an attempt to remove the lens without subluxation, but the lens nucleus continued to sink at least the inferior pole into the vitreous. This may have been associated with posterior capsule weakening from the patient's previous vitrectomy surgery. It was deemed prudent to abort the procedure and place an implant as standard policy, and to refer the patient to a retinal specialist to perform a repeat vitrectomy and lensectomy in the vitreous cavity to reduce retinal complications.

The anterior chamber was swept to ensure that there was no vitreous anterior to the anterior lens capsule release. Hyaluronate sodium was used to inflate the anterior chamber. The incision was extended to approximately 5 mm. A 21.5–diopter silicone intraocular lens implant was placed unfolded across the chamber and was sulcus fixated. Residual viscoelastic was irrigated from the eye. The incision was closed with three interrupted 10-0 nylon sutures. The conjunctiva was draped over the wound. It was sealed at the two and ten o'clock positions with cautery. Balanced saline solution was irrigated in the anterior chamber. The implant had good fixation. The lens nucleus was partially subluxed and hinged at the 12 o'clock position, dangling into the vitreous cavity. Gentamicin, 20 mg, and dexamethasone, 4 mg, were injected subconjunctivally. One drop of a combination of dexamethasone, neomycin sulfate, and polymyxin B sulfate (Maxitrol) and one drop of 4% pilocarpine were instilled. An ocular dressing and Fox shield were applied. The patient was notified of the complication. He was awake and seemed to understand it.

How is this procedure reported?

CHAPTER 4

Radiology

OBJECTIVES

This chapter will assist in accomplishing the following objectives:

- Understand definitions pertaining to radiology services
- Understand guidelines for various subsections listed in the Radiology section of the Current Procedural Terminology (CPT®) codebook
- Learn coding tips for reporting radiology services

Introduction to Radiology

The Radiology section of the CPT codebook includes four subsections:

- Diagnostic Radiology (Diagnostic Imaging)
- Diagnostic Ultrasound
- Radiation Oncology
- Nuclear Medicine

The CPT codes listed in the Radiology section of the CPT codebook apply when radiological services are performed either by the physician or under the supervision of a physician.

Supervision and Interpretation

When a procedure that is a combination of an interventional procedure and imaging is performed, the imaging portion of the procedure is designated as "radiological supervision and interpretation." When a physician both performs the procedure and provides radiological imaging supervision and interpretation, a combination of procedure codes outside the **70000** series and imaging supervision and interpretation codes are necessary to completely report the procedure(s) performed.

Administration of Contrast Material(s)

Contrast material is commonly used for imaging enhancement. Contrast material improves visualization and evaluation of the body structure or organ studied. Some of the procedures listed in the Radiology section of the CPT codebook may be performed with or without the use of contrast material for imaging enhancement. The phrase "with contrast" used in the codes for procedures using contrast for imaging enhancement represents contrast material administered intravascularly, intra-articularly, or intrathecally. For example, brain computed tomography (CT) may be done with intravenous contrast (**70460**), without contrast (**70450**), or without contrast followed by injection of intravenous contrast (**70470**). In procedures where contrast material is always used, the CPT descriptor will not indicate that contrast material is used. For instance, intravenous pyelogram and abdominal aortogram do not list "with contrast" since contrast is an intrinsic part of the procedure. When contrast materials are administered only orally and/or rectally, the study does not qualify as "with contrast" and should be coded "without contrast." A CT scan of the abdomen with oral contrast should be coded as a CT of the abdomen without contrast (**74150**). For intra-articular injection, the appropriate joint injection code is used. If radiographic arthrography is also performed, the arthrography supervision and interpretation code for the appropriate joint (which includes fluoroscopy) is also used. If CT or magnetic resonance (MR) arthrography is performed without radiographic arthrography, the appropriate joint injection code, the appropriate CT or MR code ("with contrast" or "without followed by contrast"), and the appropriate imaging guidance code for needle placement for contrast injection would be used.

Spine examinations using CT, MR imaging, or MR angiography "with contrast" may be performed with intrathecal (within either the subarachnoid or the subdural space) or intravascular contrast injection. However, for intrathecal injection of contrast material, the injection procedure is separately reported with either code **61055** or **62284**, as appropriate. Injection of intravascular contrast material is part of the "with contrast" CT, CT angiography, MR imaging, or MR angiography procedure.

Definition of "Port" and "Block"

A *port*, often referred to as a *field*, is the area encompassed by a single radiation beam. It may be defined either on a patient's surface or inside the body. Multiple intersecting ports combine to produce the three-dimensional treatment volume.

A *block* is a radiation-shielding device placed into the beam that allows for a change in the shape or projected configuration of the port. It may be a simple multiuse device that is placed by hand, a custom-designed block that is inserted on the linear accelerator, or a physician-designed multileaf collimator pattern generated by the physician utilizing a computer.

Interventional Radiology

Interventional radiology is the branch of medicine that diagnoses and/or treats a wide range of diseases by using percutaneous or minimally invasive techniques with imaging guidance. Understanding how to code for interventional radiology services requires a thorough knowledge of anatomy and physiology as well as an in-depth knowledge of the use of CPT codes unique to this specialty.

Often diagnostic and therapeutic services are delivered in a variety of combinations and permutations determined by the underlying disease process, the clinical evaluation of the patient, and the intraprocedural interpretation of the diagnostic portion of the service (including physiologic data and images obtained). These contingencies may result in several coding possibilities.

Radiation Oncology

A course of radiation therapy is composed of six steps that involve distinct activities of varying complexity. A clinical team, led by the radiation oncologist, provides the medical services associated with the steps in the process of care. Other team members in the patient's planning and treatment regimen include the medical physicist, dosimetrist, radiation therapist, and nursing staff. Many of the procedures within each step will be carried to completion before the patient's care is taken to the next step. Others will occur and reoccur during the course of treatment. Each of these distinct steps involves medical evaluation, interpretation, management, and decision making by the radiation oncologist. Certain steps, of necessity, are repeated during treatment because of patient tolerance, changes in tumor size, necessity for boost field or port size changes, protection of normal tissue, or as other clinical circumstances may require.

Steps in the course of radiation therapy are as follows.

1 **Consultation.** The radiation oncologist will have an initial encounter with the patient to evaluate the patient's history and clinical status and to ascertain whether the patient is a candidate for radiation therapy. This initial consultation is reported with Evaluation and Management (E/M) codes from the CPT codebook. Recommendations may also be made about other aspects of cancer care, eg, pain and/or nutrition management and diagnostic testing for staging.

2 **Tumor Mapping and Clinical Treatment Planning.** If the determination is made that the patient should receive radiation treatment, clinical treatment planning occurs. In this step, the disease bearing area(s) is determined and a treatment plan is devised, including the type of radiation to be used, area(s) to be treated, technique(s) for treatment, dose to be delivered, and duration of therapy. In developing the clinical treatment plan, the radiation oncologist may use information obtained from the patient's initial clinical evaluation at the time of consultation (reported with the appropriate E/M code) and review the imaging and/or lab tests to determine the treatment volume as well as critical structures in close juxtaposition to the treatment area. Consideration is also made of toxicities and tolerances associated with definitive radiation therapy or combined-modality therapy. Thereafter, the radiation oncologist is able to select the final treatment modality(ies) appropriate for the patient. The radiation oncologist may find it necessary to order additional tests, studies, or procedures to complete the planning phase. The studies that are ordered as part of clinical treatment planning may not be associated with studies necessary for staging of the cancer, but are studies that give specific information for treatment planning. The planning process becomes the foundation upon which subsequent decisions are made. CPT codes corresponding to clinical treatment planning are codes **77261–77263**.

3 **Simulation.** After the completion of clinical treatment planning, including tumor mapping, it is necessary to actually establish the treatment portals to deliver the radiation to the volume selected. Therapeutic radiology simulation is the process of establishing radiation treatment portals that most efficiently and precisely encompass the treatment volume. Simulation is usually performed on a dedicated simulator, but it can be performed on other pieces of equipment, such as virtual reality-based, three-dimensional simulation systems or other dedicated diagnostic x-ray, MR, ultrasound, or nuclear medicine equipment that is modified to localize treatment volume to define the area that requires treatment. Each portal, or port, is visualized in reference to appropriate landmarks. Each port is confirmed to encompass the desired treatment volume. Documentation of the size, angle, distance, and

other working parameters of each portal are recorded. In most instances, simulation films of each portal are recorded for future comparison with therapeutic portal images (port films) made during treatment. Under certain circumstances, a treatment unit may be used to create images for port setting (simulation is also used for determination of radioactive implant location within the body). Simulation may be performed more than once during a course of therapy, but only once per day.

4 **Medical Radiation Physics, Dosimetry, Treatment Devices, and Special Services.** This phase of the process of care involves the radiation oncologist in collaboration with the medical physicist, dosimetrist, and radiation therapist staff. This team develops dosimetry, builds treatment devices to modify and refine treatment delivery, and performs other special services required for the measurement of precision dose delivery (including quality assurance and the identification and review of complicated situations requiring special medical physics consultation). The CPT codes used are in the **77300–77399** series. The physician must prescribe, supervise, design, review, and clinically confirm all work done in this step of the process of care, including basic dosimetry calculations, isodose plans, electron beam calculations, and special dosimetry. The physician must prescribe, supervise, design, and review all work done on each aspect in these steps.

5 **Radiation Treatment Delivery and Radiation Treatment Management.** Radiation treatment delivery described by CPT codes **77401–77416** and **77520–77525** are technical codes only, and describe the delivery of external beam radiation therapy. Brachytherapy CPT codes (interstitial implants) are described in the **77750–77799** series and include both professional work and technical reimbursement.

While the patient is undergoing radiation therapy, the radiation oncologist is responsible for the care of the patient and the overall management of the course of treatment. External beam services, reported by codes **77427**, **77431**, **77432**, and **77470**, are used depending on the complexity and modality of treatment. For external beam radiation therapy, radiation therapy management is reported in units of five fractions or treatment sessions.

The professional services furnished during the treatment management typically consist of the following:

- Review of port films
- Review and modification of dosimetry, dose delivery, and treatment parameters
- Review of treatment setup
- Examination of the patient for medical evaluation and management

The management of brachytherapy treatment is included in the brachytherapy code.

6 **Patient Follow-up.** This final step in the course of radiation therapy is covered by CPT E/M codes for follow-up evaluation of an established patient. This phase involves periodic patient visits and examinations. These services

are performed after a course of radiation therapy is completed. Follow-up exams within 90 days of completion of therapy (the global period) are considered part of treatment management and are not reported separately. However, diagnostic tests such as endoscopy furnished within the 90-day global period are reported separately. If a patient returns within the 90-day global period with a new or different clinical problem, a new and separate E/M code may be reported. After the completion of the 90-day global period, usual and customary use of the CPT E/M codes for follow-up evaluation of an established patient is appropriate.

EXAMPLE

On what occasion (when) can therapeutic radiology treatment planning codes (**77261–77263**) be coded? How many times per course of treatment should treatment planning codes be used? Should these codes be reported at the beginning of treatment?

Therapeutic radiology treatment planning, as described by codes **77261**, **77262**, and **77263**, is a process of developing a "course of action" for treating a patient's disease and involves numerous issues that the radiation oncologist must take into account, including planning for devices, simulation, choice of modality, dose, fractionation, and specific anatomic constraints. Treatment planning is typically performed once for each course of therapy, and generally takes place before the treatment or simulation.

There may be occasions when a patient under therapy develops a new and unexpected problem that requires another course of therapy to a different site and for a different problem. Therefore, a change in clinical circumstances or diagnosis may require a new treatment plan.

However, it would not be appropriate to use multiple codes in the **77261–77263** series for a change in treatment plan or treatment of multiple sites for the same diagnosis and circumstance.

EXAMPLE

Do basic radiation dosimetry calculation (**77300**) and intensity modulated radiotherapy planning (**77301**) codes include clinical treatment planning (**77261–77263**) and/or therapeutic radiology simulation-aided field setting codes (**77280–77299**)? Are these codes reported each time?

Basic dosimetry (**77300**) is used in many different scenarios requiring delivery of a prescribed dose of radiation to a particular region. Multiple unique treatment ports to the same site or to different sites will each require separate calculations, as will off-axis or gap calculations. In brachytherapy, point doses and radioisotope decay may require multiple or repeated calculations.

The work described by CPT code **77300** is a distinct medical service, separate from **77301**. Code **77300** is often used with complicated computer isodose planning for external beam radiation and implants. It is appropriately reported with all other planning codes, including **77305**, **77310**, and **77315**, and is warranted with intensity-modulated radiotherapy (IMRT) planning when medically necessary. To be clear, the calculations performed to determine treatment unit settings for IMRT planning are no different than for the previously mentioned isodose plan codes **77305**, **77310**, and **77315**; accordingly, code **77300** can be reported with **77301**.

Basic radiation dosimetry calculation (CPT code **77300**) is a mathematical computation of the radiation dose at a particular point, or other independent calculations performed by a qualified medical dosimetrist, qualified medical physicist, physician, or other individual. Any further dosimetry calculation that is performed because of a change in one of the initial calculation parameters (eg, port size or shape, depth dose, blocking factor, tumor dose) is separately reportable.

Clinical treatment planning (**77261–77263**) is a separate and distinct process that takes place before simulation, dose calculation, or any radiation treatment procedure, including IMRT. It is never included in any other procedures. (See the previous discussion.)

Simulation (**77280–77290**) and dose calculations (**77300**) may be performed before or after IMRT treatment planning (**77301**) as medically required.

Following is an example of code **77300** being reported several times per course of treatment, or as many times as the physician makes the calculation.

EXAMPLE

In a four-port box treatment of the pelvis, the anterior and posterior opposed ports and the right and left lateral opposed ports are treated. If the anterior and posterior ports are identical in size, shape, and depth, they are considered to be one calculation. The same holds true for the lateral ports. Therefore, two **77300** calculations would be performed. If these same treatment ports are reduced in size later in the treatment course to accommodate tumor shrinkage or patient tolerance, it would require new dose calculations and additional uses of code **77300**.

EXAMPLE

Provide clarifying language for the terms "simple," "intermediate," and complex blocks as listed in CPT codes **77332**, **77333**, and **77334**.

77332 Treatment devices, design and construction; simple (simple block, simple bolus)

77333 Treatment devices, design and construction; intermediate (multiple blocks, stents, bite blocks, special bolus)

77334 Treatment devices, design and construction; complex (irregular blocks, special shields, compensators, wedges, molds or casts)

The level of complexity of a treatment device may be related to the clinical reason for the device or the method of construction. Not all devices are blocks. An example of a *simple* treatment device (**77332**) might be a prefabricated reusable block selected by the physician for a particular indication. An *intermediate* treatment device (**77333**) is appropriate when multiple such reusable blocks are used. The code for complex devices (**77334**) is reserved for those cases in which a highly complex field is required and a unique device is constructed for treatment or protection of sensitive vital tissues. A complex device is unique to a particular patient and port. Examples of complex devices would be a mantle field block, head and neck treatment blocks, and a custom fabricated immobilization device.

The construction of anteroposterior (AP) and posteroanterior (PA) blocks for parallel opposed beams, in which the patient does not move, the treatment machine is swung 180° to the opposed port, and the blocks are constructed from the same simulation image and are identical except for being reversed as to the location, is designated as a single set of blocks. In this example, a single charge is made for their design and professional supervision of the complex device (**77334-26**) and two charges are made for the technical reimbursement for the fabrication of the treatment devices (2 x **77334-TC**). An example of where charges for a multiple set of blocks can be rendered is a treatment vignette involving a four-field box to the pelvis. In this example, one professional charge would be made for the AP and PA blocks and another for the right and left lateral blocks (2 x **77334-26**) and code **77334-TC** would be charged four times, once for each of the ports.

If a patient has some combination of simple and intermediate treatment devices, such as a bolus, or a reusable field block covering the same treatment portal, this should be reported as a single complex treatment device rather than a separate charge for each item. In some situations, separate charges can be made for two or more complex devices that are unique and specially constructed for the patient.

Chapter 4

Radiology Exercises

EXERCISE 1

History: Right shoulder pain and instability

Procedure: The plans, risks and benefits of shoulder joint injection were discussed with the patient and he elected to proceed. With sterile technique and fluoroscopic guidance, the right glenohumeral joint was punctured with a 22-gauge spinal needle. Needle position was confirmed by injection of iodinated contrast, and then approximately 20 cc of a mixture of saline, gadolinium, and iodinated contrast was injected into the joint. No complications were noted.

Impression: Uncomplicated joint injection for radiographic arthrography and MR arthrogram.

How is this procedure reported?

EXERCISE 2

Right Shoulder Arthrogram

Procedure: For the conventional arthrogram, scout radiographs were obtained before joint injection. Additional images were obtained after joint injection. The scout views demonstrated no osseous abnormality. There was no extravasation of contrast into the subacromial/subdeltoid bursa to suggest rotator cuff tear. There was no other arthrographic abnormality.

Impression: Negative right shoulder arthrogram

How is this procedure reported?

CODING TIP

Medicare and other third-party payer guidelines should be referenced for the coding of the use of contrast.

EXERCISE 3

MR Imaging of Right Shoulder With Contrast

Procedure: After conventional arthrography, the patient was taken for MR imaging with T1, T2, and fat-suppressed sequences obtained in axial, oblique coronal, and sagittal projections. The supraspinatus and other rotator cuff tendons were normal. The glenoid labrum and capsule were normal. No osseous lesion was identified.

Impression: Negative MR examination of the right shoulder with contrast

How is this procedure reported?

EXERCISE 4

CT of Abdomen

History: Recurrent diverticulitis; transvaginal hysterectomy in the remote past for reported cervical carcinoma

Procedure: Oral contrast was given, and 120 cc of Omnipaque 350 was power injected *intravenously* without complication. Images were obtained from the diaphragm to the iliac crest. The visualized portions of the lower thorax were unremarkable. The liver, gallbladder, spleen, pancreas, and kidneys were normal in appearance. There was minimal adrenal hyperplasia bilaterally. Intra-abdominal portions of the bowel were normal in appearance. There was no mass, lymphadenopathy, or ascites in the abdomen. There was a small hiatal hernia.

Impression: Small hiatal hernia; minimal bilateral adrenal hyperplasia

How is this procedure reported?

EXERCISE 5

CT of Pelvis

Procedure: Oral contrast was given, and 120 cc of Omnipaque 350 was power injected *intravenously* without complication. Images were obtained from the iliac crest to the symphysis pubis. There was marked diverticulosis of the sigmoid colon and rectum. There was no evidence of mass, stricture, or paracolic fluid collection to suggest diverticulitis. The uterus was not seen, which was compatible with a prior hysterectomy. The bladder was normal in appearance. There were phleboliths in the pelvic vessels.

Impression: Marked diverticulosis of the sigmoid colon and rectum, without evidence of diverticulitis; status posthysterectomy

How is this procedure reported?

EXERCISE 6

History: After a previous and separate evaluation in the interventional radiology clinic for progressive lifestyle-limiting claudication of the right lower extremity, for treatment of which an aggressive exercise program failed, a 59-year-old white male former smoker presented for diagnostic arteriography and endovascular intervention.

Procedure: Because of a markedly diminished right groin pulse, the left groin was used for access. After sterile preparation and local anesthesia with 1% lidocaine, 19-gauge needle access was obtained into the left common femoral artery in a retrograde direction. Over a 0.035-in diameter wire, a 4 French pigtail catheter was advanced into the suprarenal abdominal aorta. Digital subtraction abdominal aortography was performed. The catheter was then pulled down to above the level of the aortic bifurcation and bilateral oblique pelvic angiography was performed, followed by lower-extremity angiography down to the level of the feet.

The catheter was exchanged for a 4 French Cobra catheter, which was used to selectively catheterize the right common iliac artery and then, with the assistance of a hydrophilic wire, cross the stenosis into the distal external iliac artery. Over an exchange-length stiff wire, a 6 French flexible sheath was advanced into the proximal right external iliac artery. A bolus of heparin was administered intra-arterially.

CODING TIP

Unlike most open surgical procedures, interventional radiology makes use of component coding, which allows the use of a specific combination of CPT codes to precisely describe the service provided. While this allows for very specific and accurate use of codes, it does require the coder to carefully evaluate the dictated report and identify the distinct component services that were provided.

CODING TIP

Interventional radiology vascular catheterization coding requires a detailed understanding of both arterial and venous anatomy. Coders involved with such services should make liberal use of appropriate anatomic diagrams designed specifically for interventional radiology coding (eg, to identify a vessel as a first-, second-, or third-order vessel).

CODING TIP

When the radiopharmaceutical(s) used for the procedure are reported, the HCPCS code description and the administered dose must be carefully considered. For example, if two doses are administered during a dual isotope study, one at stress with one agent and one at rest with a different agent, two HCPCS codes and units per the descriptions should be reported on the claim form.

To facilitate stent placement, the critical external iliac stenosis was predilated with a 4 mm x 4 cm angioplasty balloon. An 8 mm x 4 cm self-expanding nitinol stent was then deployed across the right external iliac artery stenosis. Repeat angiography was performed through the sheath. Stent apposition to the vessel wall was optimized by means of a 9 mm x 4 mm angioplasty balloon. Angiography was repeated once again. Simultaneous intra-arterial pressure measurements were obtained both above and below the stented region. The sheath was removed and hemostasis was achieved with manual compression.

A single renal artery was present bilaterally, without evidence of stenosis. Only mild infrarenal aortic atherosclerotic irregularity was present. The left iliac system was widely patent. The right common and internal iliac arteries were widely patent. A tighter than 95% diameter reduction stenosis is present in the mid-right external iliac artery, measuring approximately 2 cm in length.

Mild superficial femoral artery irregularity was present bilaterally, without hemodynamically significant stenosis. The profunda femoral and popliteal arteries were patent. Patent three-vessel runoff was present bilaterally without stenosis. The dorsalis pedis and posterior tibial arteries were patent in the foot.

After endovascular stent placement, no residual stenosis was present. No measurable pressure gradient was present. There was no angiographic evidence of distal embolization.

Impression: Critical right external iliac artery stenosis with excellent response to endovascular stent placement

How is this procedure reported?

EXERCISE 7

A 67-year-old male with known coronary heart disease was referred for evaluation of recent increasing angina. A resting myocardial perfusion single photon emission CT (SPECT) study was performed at 4 PM after injection of 3.0 mCi of thallous chloride. The following morning, a treadmill stress test was done under the supervision of the nuclear medicine physician; at peak exercise, 29.6 mCi of technetium Tc 99m tetrofosmin (Myoview) was administered, and a gated myocardial perfusion SPECT study was done with both wall motion and ejection fraction analysis. Imaging data were analyzed from digital display on both days. The stress imaging data were compared to the rest study results, and the complete study to a previous similar study performed 14 months previously. The patient had no cardiac symptoms during the cardiac stress procedure, which was reported separately; he reached 85% of predicted maximum heart rate. The electrocardiogram stress test tracing was sent to the patient's cardiologist for interpretation and reporting.

How is this procedure reported?

EXERCISE 8

A 68-year-old male had a history of prostate cancer and recent increasing lower back pain. Three hours after injection of 22 mCi of techentium Tc 99 m medronate (MDP), whole-body planar images were acquired from the patient's head to his feet. A SPECT study of the lumbar spine in the region of his pain was then performed. The imaging data were interpreted from digital display and hard copy, and were compared to bone x-rays of his back and pelvis acquired the previous week.

How is this procedure reported?

CHAPTER 5

Medicine

OBJECTIVES

This chapter will assist in accomplishing the following objectives:

- Identify the variety of Current Procedural Terminology (CPT®) codes used for reporting services provided by many different types of healthcare providers
- Identify services and procedures provided by nonphysician healthcare providers
- Identify procedure-oriented subsections
- Identify medical-specialty subsections

Introduction to Medicine

The Medicine section of the CPT codebook is a single section, similar to the Surgery section, and includes a variety of codes for reporting procedures and services provided by many different types of health care providers. In addition, many services and procedures provided by nonphysician health care providers can be found in the Medicine section. For example, codes in the Physical Medicine and Rehabilitation subsection are often used to report the services and procedures provided by physical and occupational therapists. Audiologists and speech therapists may find codes in the Special Otorhinolaryngologic Services subsection that describe some of the technical procedures and services they provide.

There are two basic types of subsections: those that are procedure oriented and those that refer to particular medical specialties. It is very important to remember that the codes in a specialty subsection, such as gastroenterology, are not limited to use by gastroenterologists. Any qualified physician or, as appropriate, qualified health care professional may use any code in the CPT codebook. The performance of the services is regulated by state practice acts for the various professions and is not determined by the American Medical Association or the CPT codebook.

Contact Lens Services and Spectacle Services

The Contact Lens Services heading of the CPT code set is somewhat unusual because, in addition to the professional services involved in the prescription and fitting of contact lenses, the CPT nomenclature contains codes for the replacement of contact lenses (**92326**), as well as including the supply of the contact lens itself as part of the overall prescription and fitting service.

Another unique characteristic of this section is that many of the codes differentiate between a patient's condition for aphakia and other than aphakia. *Aphakia* is defined as absence of the lens of the eye. The most common cause of this condition is surgical removal of the lens because of cataracts. Aphakia may also be due to absorption or degeneration of the lens or, very rarely, congenital absence of the lens.

When codes are selected for contact lens and spectacle services, the code should be chosen on the basis of whether the physician actually provides the lenses or supervises the fitting by an independent technician.

Reporting Services for Contact Lenses

The provision of eye care, and the mechanisms to report that care, have evolved with different methods to report many of the services and materials involved. This can be challenging to code for both the provider and the coder, especially since reporting requirements may vary among third-party payers.

Third-party payers frequently address eye care in two categories:

- Eye care noncovered by the patient's major medical insurance or covered by "vision care" insurance
- Eye care covered by major medical insurance

The CPT codebook includes codes for intermediate and comprehensive ophthalmologic services, which are special codes that describe the unique nature of ophthalmologic examinations (**92002–92014**). These codes may overlap with the general Evaluation and Management (E/M) codes (**99201–99215**), depending on the specific services provided to the patient.

The E/M codes may be used by any physician, including ophthalmologists or optometrists, to report an office evaluation. However, codes **92002–92014** share several definitions with the E/M codes, such as new and established patient, and may also be used to report the same services rendered in the ophthalmology or optometry office. Differing from the E/M codes, the general ophthalmologic services describe the physician's activity as intermediate and comprehensive and do not follow the E/M framework of the three key components of history, examination, and medical decision making, or use the documentation guidelines of the Center for Medicare and Medicaid Services to determine the proper code selection. The nature of ophthalmic examinations justified the development of codes **92002–92014**, and they are an important part of appropriately reporting ophthalmologic services.

The supply of ophthalmic materials is another example of various reporting methods.

There are options for reporting the supply of contact lens materials to the third-party payer:

- CPT guidelines allow for the inclusion of the lens materials within the prescription code. CPT coding instructions at the beginning of the Contact Lens Services heading instruct the coder that the supply of contact lenses may be reported as part of the service of fitting in the prescription code.
- If the supply of the contact lenses is not included by the practitioner in the service of fitting, code **92391** for nonaphakic patients or code **92396** for aphakic patients should be reported separately, with modifier 26 appended to report the professional services without inclusion of the materials.
- Alternatively, Healthcare Common Procedure Coding System (HCPCS) Level II codes are available for reporting of materials including contact lenses. Many third-party payers require the use of these codes for reporting supplies and materials.

Reporting requirements for these codes may vary among third-party payers, as individual payers may have specific reporting and reimbursement policies. The coder should contact the appropriate third-party payer for its requirements when reporting these codes.

Special Otorhinolaryngologic Services

Evaluative and Therapeutic Services

The Evaluative and Therapeutic Services code range (**92601–92617**) includes codes for reporting diagnostic analysis for cochlear implants, evaluation and therapeutic services for augmentative and alternative communication devices, evaluation of oral and pharyngeal swallowing function, motion fluoroscopic evaluation and flexible fiberoptic endoscopic evaluation of swallowing, and laryngeal sensory testing. Parenthetic notes and guidelines are included to help instruct the user toward the intent and use of the codes described in this subheading. Codes **92612–92617** include services that include reporting by the speech-language pathologist and physician interpretation and report only.

A View of the Outer Cochlear Implant

92601–92604

An example of the elements which are addressed in the diagnostic analysis and reprogramming of the cochlear implant.

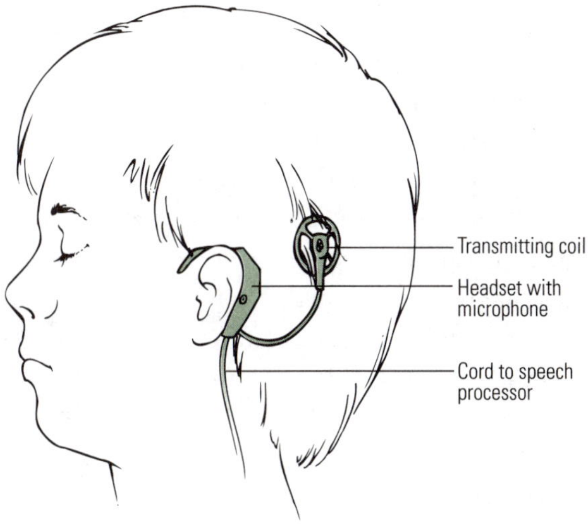

Allergy and Clinical Immunology

Allergy sensitivity tests describe the performance and reading of selective cutaneous and mucous membrane tests in correlation with the history, physical examination, and other observations of the patient. The number of tests performed should be judicious and dependent on the history, physical findings, and clinical judgment of the practitioner. Not all patients should necessarily receive the same tests or the same number of sensitivity tests.

Immunotherapy (desensitization, hyposensitization) is the parenteral administration of allergenic extracts as antigens at periodic intervals, usually on an increasing dosage scale, to a dose that is selected as maintenance therapy. Office or other outpatient visits may be reported in addition to allergen immunotherapy only when other significant identifiable services are provided with the immunotherapy. If allergen immunotherapy is the only service provided, an office visit code should not be reported.

Neurostimulators, Analysis-Programming

Complex neurostimulators are clinically available and effective in managing patients with neurological disorders. Neurostimulator codes were established to differentiate the time and effort associated with evaluation, testing, programming, or reprogramming of neurostimulator systems. Deep brain stimulation is used to treat movement disorders (eg, rigidity, tremors, balance control). For example, with the electrode array placed in the thalamus, stimulation is used for treatment of essential tremor or tremor resulting from Parkinson disease. A deep brain stimulator can also be placed in the globus pallidus or subthalamic nucleus for Parkinson disease, essential tremor, and other conditions such as multiple sclerosis. With the array placed in these locations, several clinical features, such as rigidity, dyskinesia, and/or tremor, can be treated. When several clinical features are treated, the evaluation and monitoring of the patient's reaction to each stimulation setting is a complex process. This is in part due to the need for repeated, very detailed neurologic testing, including difficulty in determining the most appropriate stimulation setting, as a given setting revision may improve one feature (eg, rigidity) but actually worsen another (eg, dyskinesia). The CPT guidelines differentiate between a simple and a complex neurostimulator

A simple neurostimulator pulse generator/transmitter is capable of affecting or changing three or fewer of the following features: pulse amplitude; pulse duration; pulse frequency; eight or more electrode contacts; cycling (meaning automatic on and off for different times in microseconds); stimulation train duration; train spacing; number of programs; number of channels; alternating electrode polarities; dose time (stimulation parameters changing in periods of minutes, including dose lockout times); and more than one clinical feature (eg, rigidity, dyskinesia, tremor).

A complex neurostimulator pulse generator/transmitter is one capable of affecting more than three of the above features.

The stimulation programming codes are based on what the system is capable of affecting and not on what parameters are being utilized for programming at any given programming session. For example, programming of thalamic deep brain stimulation is indeed only simple programming. The reason is that only one clinical feature (ie, tremor) is mainly, if not entirely, affected by stimulation in this location. It is true that "tremor" can occur in different body positions, at different times, and have different forms, etc, but ultimately it is still only one clinical feature that is being treated. Stimulation in the globus pallidus or subthalamic nucleus, on the other hand, affects multiple different clinical features, such as tremor, rigidity, or dyskinesia.

Health and Behavior Assessment/Intervention

Many services performed by psychologists and other nonphysician (ie, non-doctor of osteopathy [DO]/doctor of medicine [MD]) practitioners are performed to enhance a patient's overall health. This includes, but is not limited to, a number of types of psychotherapy services, as well as other mental health procedures intended to treat designated, diagnosed mental illness. Sometimes, however, these services are offered to a patient who presents with established illnesses or symptoms who are not diagnosed with mental illnesses. Instead of treating a particular illness, these services are intended to assess and address certain factors related to the patient's physical health. These factors can include modification in a patient's behavior toward prevention, treatment, or management of the physical health problem, or other factors that do not directly treat a diagnosed illness but affect recovery or its progression.

For patients who can benefit from this type of treatment, the assessment may focus on factors related to the patient's physical health, which may include assisting a patient in changing his or her behavioral habits for taking medication, managing and expressing symptoms, or eliminating behaviors that exacerbate the symptoms.

The psychiatry codes (**90801–90899**) refer to psychotherapy, psychological testing, and psychiatric evaluation, and all require a mental health diagnosis. In most cases, difficulties associated with an acute or chronic illness, prevention of a physical illness or disability, and maintenance of health do not meet criteria for a psychiatric diagnosis. Use of the Health and Behavior Assessment/Intervention codes eliminates inappropriate labeling of the patient as having a mental health disorder when the problem is actually a physical illness.

These codes may be reported by, but are not limited to, psychologists, advanced practice nurses, clinical social workers, and other nonphysician health care professionals within their scope of practice who have specialty or subspecialty training in health and behavior assessment/intervention procedures. These codes are *not* intended to be used by physicians. Instead, physicians performing these services may identify their efforts by choosing the E/M codes appropriate to the type and level of service being provided, using the key components (ie, history, examination, medical decision making) to identify the level of service provided or, when counseling/coordination of care represent 50% or more of the total time spent for the visit, using time for choosing the appropriate E/M code.

These services are inherently identified as face-to-face services. Therefore, questionnaires given to the patient without face-to-face contact should not be reported with these codes. In addition, these services do not include neuropsychological testing. Separate codes should be used to identify this service if performed. If psychiatric services are required (such as psychotherapy services), then the predominant service (eg, psychotherapy) should be reported instead.

Health and Behavior Assessment/Intervention codes are not intended to represent preventive medicine services, as these services do not identify the comprehensive evaluation services as identified in the Preventive Medicine Services codes. If comprehensive evaluation services are performed, then these codes (**99381–99397**) should be used to identify those specific services. These codes should not be reported on the same day, in addition to Preventive Medicine Counseling and/or Risk Factor Reduction Intervention services (**99401–99412**).

> **CODING TIP**
>
> The supervised modalities (**97010–97028**) do not require direct (one-on-one) patient contact by the provider. Also, these are reported only once per session or as one unit of a code per session, regardless of the number of body parts receiving application of that modality.

Physical Medicine and Rehabilitation

Physical Medicine and Rehabilitation codes (**97000** series) are not restricted to use by a specific specialty group. They may be used by any provider who is qualified to perform the service represented by the specific code. No distinction is made concerning the licensure or professional credentials of the provider. Licensure varies on a state-by-state basis, and credentialing varies on an institutional basis. Relevant state and institutional authorities should be consulted regarding the appropriate provision of these services by health care professionals.

Codes **97001–97004** are used to report physical and occupational therapy evaluation and reevaluation. These codes identify a dynamic process in which clinical judgments are made on the basis of data gathered. These evaluations result in the development of a plan for management of a patient's problems as they relate to his or her disease or disability. Codes **97005** and **97006** describe athletic training evaluation and reevaluation, respectively.

Because some of the physical medicine services include an evaluation component as part of preservice work, use of these codes is dependent on whether the service being provided is a significant, separate service, or simply a component of the more involved procedure. And as patient circumstances vary, deciding when to use these codes depends on the specific patient encounter and identifying what has actually been done.

Supervised modality codes (**97010–97028**) are for the application of a modality that does not require direct (one-on-one) patient contact by the provider. Conversely, constant attendance modality codes are for the application of a modality that requires direct (one-on-one) patient contact by the provider.

Time frames indicated in the descriptor language of the constant attendance modality codes describe the total time, ie, preservice, intraservice, and postservice time spent in performing this modality. Supervised modality codes that do not include an increment of time in the descriptor do not use time as a component for determining the use of the code. The code is reported without regard to the length of time spent performing the service.

Medical Nutrition Therapy

Medical nutrition therapy (MNT) includes nutritional diagnostic therapy and counseling services provided by a registered dietitian (RD) or licensed nutrition professional for the purpose of managing disease. Medical nutrition therapy occurs over multiple encounters. The typical MNT service includes the initial assessment and intervention followed by multiple reassessment and intervention encounters. For chronic diseases, annual follow-up MNT encounters are scheduled.

The CPT codes for MNT are used in sequence, starting with the initial MNT assessment and intervention, with subsequent use of MNT CPT codes for either individual or group reassessment and intervention.

Osteopathic Manipulative Treatment

Osteopathic manipulative treatment (OMT) is reported with codes in the **98925–98929** series. Osteopathic manipulative treatment is a form of manual treatment applied by a physician to eliminate or alleviate somatic dysfunction and related disorders. This treatment may be accomplished by a variety of techniques. Osteopathic manipulative treatment refers to more than 20 different manual treatment techniques. The procedures may be used by DOs and MDs.

Evaluation and Management services may be separately reported if, and only if, the patient's condition requires a significant separately identifiable E/M service, above and beyond the usual preservice and postservice work associated with the procedure. In this case, modifier 25 would be appended to the E/M code reported. The E/M service may be caused or prompted by the same symptoms or condition for which the OMT service was provided. Therefore, different diagnoses are not required for the reporting of OMT and E/M on the same date.

The codes for OMT are reported on the basis of the number of body regions involved. The body regions referred to are head, cervical, thoracic, lumbar, sacral, pelvic, lower extremities, upper extremities, rib cage, abdomen, and viscera.

Chiropractic Manipulative Treatment

Codes **98940–98943** are used to report chiropractic manipulative treatment (CMT). Chiropractic manipulative treatment is a form of manual treatment to influence joint and neurophysiologic function and can be accomplished through the use of a variety of techniques. Chiropractic adjustment is a therapeutic procedure that uses (1) controlled force, (2) leverage, (3) direction, (4) amplitude, and (5) velocity, which is directed at specific joints or anatomical regions. CMT takes into account a variety of factors, including subluxation. *Subluxation* is a motion segment in which the alignment, movement integrity, and/or physiologic function are altered although contact between joint surfaces remains intact.

Chiropractic is a health care discipline that emphasizes the inherent recuperative power of the body without the use of drugs or surgery. This is accomplished by focusing on the relationship between structure, primarily the spine, and function, as coordinated by the nervous system, as that relationship may affect the preservation and restoration of health.

The complete service of chiropractic manipulation requires a certain amount of preservice and intraservice work that is included as part of the service. This evaluation and management is necessary to determine not only what specific work will be necessary, but also the effectiveness of the service being provided.

Preservice work includes reviewing previously gathered clinical data (including an initial or interim history, reviewing the problem list, pertinent correspondence or reports, and other important findings and prior care), review of imaging and other test results, test interpretation, and care planning.

Intraservice work includes an interactive patient reassessment, ie, determining the current status, determining indicators/contraindications, assessing the change in condition, evaluating any new complaints, correlating physical findings, and coordinating and modifying the current treatment plan. Also included in the intraservice work is a number of manipulation and postadjustment assessments that are necessary to adequately treat the ailment presented. This work is inherently included as part of the CMT service and would not be coded separately. If additional E/M services are performed, they may be reported separately by appending modifier 25, if and only if the patient's condition requires a significant, separately identifiable E/M service above and beyond the usual preservice and postservice work associated with the procedure.

For purposes of CMT, there are spinal regions and extraspinal regions to consider. The five spinal regions referred to are listed here:

- Cervical region (includes atlanto-occipital joint)
- Thoracic region (includes costovertebral and costotransverse joints)
- Lumbar region
- Sacral region
- Pelvic (sacroiliac joint) region

The five extraspinal regions referred to are listed here:

- Head (including temporomandibular joint, excluding the atlanto-occipital region)
- Lower extremities
- Upper extremities
- Rib cage (excluding costotransverse and costovertebral joints)
- Abdomen

Chapter 5

Medicine Exercises

Contact Lens Services Exercises

EXERCISE 1

A 25-year-old male, established patient with complaints of itching eyes with reduced vision was evaluated in the office. The patient's history included seasonal allergies with treatment with oral over-the-counter allergy medications, and he had a family history of kerataconus. The reduced vision has been noticeable for about 6 months. There was no history of ocular trauma.

Refraction showed decreased myopia and increased astigmatism OU (in both eyes). Examination revealed moderate allergic conjunctivitis and mild giant papillary conjunctivitis, thinning of the central cornea, and development of a central cone OU. A Hudson-Stali line was observed OU.

Best-corrected visual acuity with spectacles was 20/50 OD (right eye) and 20/60 OS (left eye). Keratometry demonstrated significant corneal distortion, and topography showed a typical kerataconus pattern OU. Pachymetry confirmed significant thinning of the central cornea OU.

After discussing the options with the patient, the physician recommended fitting with rigid gas-permeable contact lenses. Additionally, topical ocular medications were prescribed to help control the symptoms of allergic conjunctivitis. The relatively early stage of the kerataconus allowed for the fitting of a standard-design rigid gas-permeable contact lenses rather than a more complex kerataconus lens. The patient was trained in insertion, removal, wearing schedule, lens and case hygiene, and normal and abnormal symptoms.

The patient returned to the office at one week, per instructions. Acuity, lens fit, corneal integrity, comfort, and patient compliance were evaluated and discussed. Any adjustments deemed necessary to the original fit of the lenses were ordered. A subsequent visit was scheduled for two weeks later.

How is this procedure reported?

EXERCISE 2

A 20-year-old male, new patient returned after surgery to repair a penetrating injury of the OD. The injury resulted in physiologic lens extraction, substantial damage to the iris and lens capsule, and a large peripheral corneal scar. A small peripheral retinal detachment had been repaired and appeared reattached. The surgeon was unable to place an intraocular implant in the eye. A review of history disclosed no other significant systemic history. The eye was quiet and completely healed from the surgery.

Corneal topography showed mild corneal distortion, significant against-the-rule astigmatism, and loss of pattern in the immediate area of the corneal scar of the OD. The OS had a typical pattern of low with-the-rule astigmatism. Corneal pachymetry confirmed that the central corneal thickness was about average at 557 microns.

Refraction, as expected, showed high anisometropia, with the OD having very high hyperopia because of the aphakia and significant astigmatism. The OS had a low myopic astigmatism prescription. There was some diplopia, through trial spectacle lenses, when the patient was not looking straight ahead.

After careful discussion of the options, the physician recommended fitting with a soft single-vision contact lenses for the OD. The patient was counseled that glasses should be worn full time for safety, for uncorrected astigmatism in the OD and for reading prescription to establish binocular vision at near.

How is this procedure reported?

Spectacle Services Exercises

EXERCISE 1

A 68-year-old male was seen for a yearly follow-up. He requested low-vision evaluation after a diagnosis of mild age-related macular degeneration. He reported having been able to read a newspaper until six months previously. The patient expressed interest in stronger glasses for the specific goal of reading newsprint. The results of the low-vision testing indicated no change in the current distance spectacle correction. The old spectacle prescription bifocal of +2.50 provided 20/60 near-point acuity at a 16-in working distance. It was determined that a +5.00 add with good illumination allowed the patient to read newsprint at good speed. The reduced working distance was acceptable and the prescription change prescribed. In the physician's opinion, it did not appear necessary to schedule therapy or follow-up.

How is this procedure reported?

EXERCISE 2

A new patient, a 24-year-old male, had never had a driver's license because of moderate visual impairment. Low-vision evaluation demonstrated that, as a result of optic nerve hypoplasia, the patient's best-corrected distance acuity measured 20/200 OD and 20/100 OS. State driver's license policy, in his state, required distance acuity of 20/40 or better and did permit driving with the use of a bioptic device after a 2-month adaptation and training period using the bioptic device. The patient demonstrated a conscientious attitude regarding driving and no physical or mental contraindications relative to driving. Visual fields were normal and acuity was stable. After a review of the limitations inherent in bioptic use and its appropriate application for driving, it was elected to proceed with bioptic prescription. Testing showed a 3.0x bioptic telescope OS to provide 20/30 distance acuity. The total face-to-face time was 80 minutes. The physician recommended a brief period of instruction and counseling at delivery of the bioptic device and additional support as needed.

How is this procedure reported?

Special Otorhinolaryngologic Services Exercises

EXERCISE 1

A patient presented with a weak, breathy vocal quality and could not initiate pitch change. He was oriented and able to make himself understood when he slowed his rate of speech and used short phrases. The speech-language pathologist assessed oral motor skills, reflexes, laryngeal function, and cognitive-communicative skills, as well as noting reduction in tongue-tip elevation, anterior-posterior tongue movement, and lip pucker/smile.

The patient was unable to trigger a volitional swallow of saliva immediately when asked, but he did swallow after several seconds. He was presented with a variety of foods of different textures to assess the oral phase of the swallow and to determine whether he had signs of pharyngeal dysphagia. Introduction of a quarter-teaspoon of puree on a spoon showed weak lip closure, decreased tongue movement, and delayed pharyngeal swallow with what appeared to be limited laryngeal elevation. The patient admitted a sensation of residue in his throat after the swallow. There were no overt signs of choking with this consistency. He also exhibited oral residue. When presented with a bite of cookie, the patient had a difficult time masticating and forming a bolus, with pocketing in the cheek and residue on the tongue after the swallow. Overt choking was evident after a quarter-teaspoon of water and after a mixed consistency (cereal with milk).

The speech-language pathologist diagnosed moderate oral dysphagia and noted the following signs of probable pharyngeal dysphagia: weak laryngeal elevation, delayed initiation of volitional swallow, choking, and questionable pharyngeal residue. Recommendations included the continued use of a nasogastric tube for nutrition, hydration, and medications, maintaining nothing by mouth (NPO) status. The patient's physician was apprised of the need for (1) continued NPO status, (2) treatment to increase strength, range, and mobility of lips and tongue and improved bolus formation and manipulation, and (3) referral for instrumental examination of the pharyngeal phase of the swallow.

The appropriate code to report is:

A. **92610** *Evaluation of oral and pharyngeal swallowing function*

B. **92611** *Motion fluoroscopic evaluation of swallowing function by cine or video recording*

C. **92612** *Flexible fiberoptic endoscopic evaluation of swallowing by cine or video recording*

EXERCISE 2

If a physician performs a flexible fiberoptic endoscopic evaluation of swallowing by video recording, reviews the videotape, interprets the findings, and writes a report, what code(s) is reported for this entire study?

Allergy and Clinical Immunology Exercises

CODING TIP

The number of percutaneous or intracutaneous tests should be specified, and the total charge is the number of tests times the cost per test.

EXERCISE 1

A patient with a suspected IgE-mediated allergic disease to an aeroallergen or food arrived in the office. Using a combination of medical history, physical examination, and knowledge of the local aerobiology, as well as the patient's environmental history, the physician selected appropriate inhalant or food allergens for testing. After determining that the patient was not acutely ill and that he had stopped taking antihistamines for an appropriate length of time, the patient was asked to remove his shirt for skin testing on his back. The skin test location was cleaned and then marked with a pen so that each extract had a specific identifiable location. Each extract was applied to its skin test site one at a time or in small groups with an appropriate device that penetrated the epidermis. At least one positive and a negative control also were applied. A timer was set and the patient waited for 15 to 20 minutes while the reactions developed. The size of each reaction's wheal and erythema was measured in millimeters, and the result was recorded on the skin test sheet. The reactions also may be categorized in terms of 0 to 4 based on the measurements. Appropriate monitoring equipment and safety measures were available during the testing. The physician reviewed the results and, after comparing them with the controls, determined which reactions were clinically significant. The patient was ascertained to be doing well before he left the office.

How is this procedure reported?

EXERCISE 2

A patient who had an anaphylactic reaction after an insect sting was referred to find out which insect caused the sting and what to do to prevent future systemic or anaphylactic episodes. Freshly reconstituted insect venom was applied to labeled areas of the skin. Through the drop of each antigen, the skin was pricked with a new bifurcated needle. The cross diameters of each wheal and flare were measured at 15 to 20 minutes and recorded on the appropriate form. The same procedure was carried out with diluent and histamine used as negative and positive controls. The physician evaluated each reaction to determine whether further testing at a higher concentration was indicated on the basis of the patient history and skin test responses.

Intracutaneous testing was performed next. The venom was drawn up in a syringe with a needle designed for intradermal testing. Each incremental dose of each antigen was injected beginning with the lowest concentration. Appropriate monitoring equipment and safety measures were available during testing. The cross diameters of each wheal and flare were measured at 15 to

20 minutes and recorded on the appropriate form. This process was continued until the reaction was positive or the highest concentration that did not produce a nonspecific (not immunologically meaningful) reaction occurred.

How is this procedure reported?

EXERCISE 3

A patient was suspected to have an immediate hypersensitivity (IgE-mediated) reaction to an inhalant allergen and had a negative percutaneous test. An intracutaneous test was performed because it was more sensitive and might detect the presence of specific IgE although the percutaneous test was negative.

How is this procedure reported?

EXERCISE 4

A patient underwent a methacholine challenge to determine whether she had airway hyperreactivity. The patient was observed throughout the procedure for adverse events, and objective criteria of pulmonary function tests were collected after each dose administered. The test was complete when the patient's forced expiratory volume in one second (FEV_1) dropped by 20% compared to the saline inhalation "baseline" or the maximum inhaled dose of methacholine was reached without a drop in FEV_1. Before the actual challenge, certain drugs were avoided and the methacholine was prepared in appropriate dilutions.

The patient first underwent pulmonary function testing to be sure that the function was in a range suitable for testing. She was challenged first with diluent solution. For diluent solution and subsequent increasing concentrations of test solution, three inhalations of the solution were done. Approximately one minute after the final inhalation at each dose level, spirometry was repeated. Appropriate monitoring equipment and safety measures were available. If the solution did not produce the required change in FEV_1, the next higher concentration was used for inhalations about five minutes after the end of the previous series of inhalations. The pulmonary function tests were repeated after this series of inhalations, until the FEV_1 fell or the maximum concentration was reached.

How is this procedure reported?

EXERCISE 5

A patient had a previous systemic reaction (possibly anaphylaxis) to penicillin and subsequently needed to be treated with penicillin. The drug was given in gradually increasing doses in a carefully controlled environment. This type of desensitization required frequent monitoring of vital signs and constant observation. Appropriate monitoring equipment and safety measures were available during the process.

How is this procedure reported?

Neurostimulators, Analysis-Programming Exercises

CODING TIP

The services provided on the same day can include both E/M services and reprogramming. The reprogramming time is inclusive of the several stages of that service, including the initial system analysis, initial reprogramming time, initial time waiting for stabilization, subsequent cycles of reprogramming and waiting for stabilization, and final counseling and instructions.

EXERCISE 1

A 53-year-old male received a deep brain stimulator bilaterally for medically refractory Parkinson disease. The patient returned to the office for reprogramming of the devices.

The system programming was checked to ensure proper functioning; the physician tested combinations of the implant parameters, while assessing the degree of symptom and side effect improvement of worsening after each programming change. Electronic analysis and programming of an implanted permanent single-array electrode system and subcutaneous generator/transmitter was performed. After each round of reprogramming, the patient waited in the office for the new stimulation therapy to take effect. After a brief wait, the stimulator was again reprogrammed to try to achieve better results. After the patient's device was programmed to achieve maximal comfortable stimulation, the physician provided the patient and family members with detailed instructions regarding stimulator operation and precautions. The overall reprogramming session, including analysis, four reprogramming sessions, three waiting periods, and final instructions took three hours. In addition, detailed history and physical examination and moderate-complexity medical decision making were provided concerning the patient's medication regimen, to address concurrent medical problems, and to counsel the patient and family about psychosocial difficulties encountered in coping with moderately advanced Parkinson disease.

How is this procedure reported?

Health and Behavior Assessment/Intervention Exercises

EXERCISE 1

Codes **96150–96155** may be reported by pediatricians, family physicians, psychiatrists, and psychologists.

True or false?

EXERCISE 2

A 5-year-old male undergoing treatment for acute lymphoblastic leukemia was referred for assessment of pain, severe behavioral distress, and combativeness associated with repeated lumbar punctures and intrathecal chemotherapy administration. Previously unsuccessful approaches included pharmacologic treatment of anxiety, conscious sedation, and chloral hydrate, which only exacerbated the child's distress as a result of partial sedation. General anesthesia was ruled out because the child's asthma increased the respiratory risk of anesthesia to unacceptable levels.

The patient was assessed by means of standardized questionnaires (eg, the Information-Seeking Scale, Pediatric Pain Questionnaire, Coping Strategies

Inventory), which, in view of the child's age, were administered in a structured format. The medical staff and child's parents were also interviewed. On the day of a scheduled medical procedure, the child completed a self-report distress questionnaire. Behavioral observations were also made during the procedure by means of the CAMPIS-R, a structured observation scale that quantifies child, parent, and medical staff behavior. The patient's condition was assessed through the administration of various health and behavior assessment instruments, which took approximately 15 minutes.

What is the appropriate code to report?

EXERCISE 3

A 42-year-old male had been diagnosed with cancer of the pancreas. He was undergoing both aggressive chemotherapy and radiation treatments. His prognosis was guarded. He was not in the end-stage disease process and therefore did not qualify for hospice care. The patient was seen initially to improve pain management via imagery, breathing exercises, and other therapeutic interventions to address quality of life, treatment options, and death and dying issues.

Because of the medical protocol and the patient's inability to travel to additional sessions between hospitalizations, a plan was developed for extending treatment at home with the patient's wife as his primary home caregiver. The health care provider trained the patient's wife in how to assist the patient in objectively monitoring his pain and in applying exercises learned via his treatment sessions to manage pain. Issues of the patient's quality of life, as well as death and dying concerns, were also addressed, and the wife was taught how to make appropriate home interventions between sessions. Effective communication with her husband's physician and other members of his treatment team regarding his treatment protocols was facilitated.

What is the appropriate code to report?

Physical Medicine and Rehabilitation Exercises

EXERCISE 1

A 48-year-old female sustained an injury to her cervical, thoracic, and lumbar spine in a motor vehicle accident. The physical therapist performed a review of all pertinent medical records, including emergency department reports, physician examination, and radiological reports before examining the patient.

After a thorough examination, history taking, systems review, and evaluation, the physical therapist determined that the patient should initiate a treatment program consisting of unattended electrical stimulation to the cervical and lumbar spine for 15 minutes each and mechanical traction to the cervical spine for 15 minutes. Soft-tissue mobilization to the cervical, thoracic, and lumbar spine regions was performed for 25 minutes.

During the final ten minutes of treatment, the patient was instructed in proper positioning and body mechanics during daily activities at home and provided with advice regarding prevention of secondary injury.

How is this procedure reported?

EXERCISE 2

A 68-year-old male with a medical diagnosis of severe osteoarthritis of the left knee had a total knee replacement with the hope of relieving pain and increasing function. After discharge from the hospital and home care services, he began outpatient physical therapy.

The physical therapist performed a review of all pertinent medical records, including physician examination and operative, hospital, and radiological reports before examining the patient.

At the time of initial examination and evaluation, the physical therapist determined that the patient had significant limitations in range of motion and strength of the left lower extremity. The patient's incision scar was adhered, causing restriction in flexion, terminal extension, and incision pain. The patient ambulated with a walker on all surfaces and was unable to climb stairs or navigate curbs.

At a subsequent visit, the physical therapist provided the following: 30 minutes of exercises to increase flexibility and strength of the left knee and 10 minutes of soft-tissue mobilization to decrease incision scar adherence. The therapist used 15 minutes to fit the patient with a standard cane and instructed the patient in its use on flat surfaces and stairs with and without railings.

At the end of the visit, the patient was provided guidelines for instituting the updated home program.

How is this procedure reported?

CODING TIP

Each patient treated in a group setting does not have to have the same diagnosis or be provided the same interventions.

EXERCISE 3

A 32-year-old male deliveryman injured his back while moving a sofa bed. After a review of all pertinent medical records, including physician examination and radiological reports, the patient received six physical therapy treatments for care of the acute injury. The goals of these treatments were to decrease pain, increase strength of trunk musculature, and restore normal movement to the spine.

Once the original goals were achieved, it was determined that the remaining goals of treatment, including instruction in proper body mechanics during functional activities and prevention of future back injury, had not been met. The patient participated in two group sessions with a physical therapist. Each session was 45 minutes in length and had three participants. During the sessions, the physical therapist instructed each participant in proper body mechanics to be used during activities such as lifting as well as strategies to prevent future injury to the low back.

After the group sessions, each patient was provided with written materials regarding injury prevention, posture, and ergonomic advice for their job setting.

How is this procedure reported?

EXERCISE 4

A 57-year-old male deliveryman required a functional capacity evaluation to determine his ability to tolerate the demands of returning to work. The physical therapist performed a review of all pertinent medical records, including physician examination, operative reports, radiological reports, and the job task analysis report before seeing the client.

The client participated in a customized functional capacity evaluation during a four-hour period on one day. The therapist collected pertinent objective and subjective data during the testing and prepared a written report.

How is this procedure reported?

Medical Nutrition Therapy Exercises

EXERCISE 1

A 67-year-old male discharged from the hospital with the diagnosis of hypertension and chronic kidney disease was referred to an RD for MNT services. These services, described as nutritional diagnostic therapy and counseling services provided by an RD or nutrition professional for the purpose of managing disease, were initiated to delay dialysis. The RD performed the nutrition assessment and intervention with the patient to establish therapeutic lifestyle changes. The patient lived alone and frequently ate meals outside the home. The MNT initial intervention targeted new behaviors. Demonstration and instruction on food portions and appropriate food selection were performed with the patient. He was asked to return in two weeks for MNT reassessment and intervention.

The RD reviewed the nutrition screen, reviewed documentation or communication from other health care professionals, and used the American Dietetic Association's publication, *MNT Evidence-Based Guide for Practice*, to perform the nutrition assessment and determine the nutrition diagnosis and appropriate intervention(s). The MNT assessment factors included the clinical assessment of laboratory studies, medications, clinical signs and symptoms, and the nutrition physical, while therapeutic lifestyle changes included, but were not limited to, the patient's food/meal planning and preparation, activity level, and readiness to learn and change behavior. Intervention was determined on the basis of the *MNT Evidence-Based Guide for Practice* and patient factors.

How is this procedure reported?

CODING TIP

Pre-MNT services vary depending on the complexity of the disease or condition, and the amount of data to review in the MNT screening and MNT assessment service time.

CODING TIP

Intra-MNT, the initial medical nutrition therapy assessment and intervention as described in the American Dietetic Association's *MNT Evidence-Based Guide for Practice*, generally involves 60 to 90 minutes of face-to-face time with the patient/client. MNT reassessment and intervention typically involves 30 to 45 minutes of face-to-face time with the patient/client.

CODING TIP

Post-MNT services, including documentation and communication with other health care providers, may vary depending on the complexity of the disease or condition.

EXERCISE 2

A 66-year-old female with preexisting osteoporosis and hyperlipidemia was diagnosed with type 2 diabetes. The patient was taking oral medication for diabetes management. She received initial MNT services provided by an RD in the outpatient setting. The patient and the RD established three therapeutic lifestyle goals: to perform blood glucose monitoring, to complete a daily food diary, and to begin counting carbohydrates at scheduled mealtimes. The patient returned for follow-up MNT services, at which time the RD reassessed the patient's nutrition self-management goals and provided additional intervention. A follow-up encounter was scheduled in two weeks.

How is this procedure reported?

EXERCISE 3

A 55-year-old male with hyperlipidemia and hypertension received outpatient individualized MNT assessment and then follow-up intervention via group MNT sessions. Group MNT consisted of five one-hour sessions. The first group session topic included identification of optimal cholesterol, low-density lipoprotein, and high-density lipoprotein levels; therapeutic lifestyle changes to modify total fat, saturated fat, trans–fatty acid, and cholesterol intakes and to increase monounsaturated and polyunsaturated fatty acid consumption; and goal setting to identify improvements in lipid parameters to be achieved.

How is this procedure reported?

Osteopathic and Chiropractic Manipulative Treatment Exercises

EXERCISE 1

A 35-year-old male came in with complaints of low back pain and neck pain that had been present for a couple of years. This was most recently aggravated by some physical activities. A brief evaluation showed that chiropractic spinal manipulative treatment was clinically indicated in two regions: the C2 cervical region; and the L4, L5 lumbar region. Chiropractic manipulation of C2 was performed. Gonstead lumbar adjustments were made.

How is this procedure reported?

EXERCISE 2

A 30-year-old administrative assistant complained of pain and weakness in the right hand and elbow that worsened throughout her workday. A brief evaluation with the chiropractor showed that CMT was clinically indicated on the right elbow and hand. Manipulation to the right elbow, the right hand, and the right wrist was performed.

How is this procedure reported?

APPENDIX

Answers to Chapter Exercises

Chapter 1

Evaluation and Management Services Answers

EXERCISE 1

Answer: Report the appropriate Office or Other Outpatient Consultations code (**99241–99245**).

Rationale for Code Selection

Remember that a consultation must include the following:

- A written or verbal request for a consultation must be made by a physician or other appropriate source and documented in the patient's medical record.
- The consultant must document his or her opinion and any services ordered or performed.
- The consultant may initiate diagnostic and/or therapeutic services at the same or a subsequent visit.
- The consultant must communicate, in a written report, the opinion and any services ordered or performed to the requesting physician or other appropriate source.

This scenario identifies a consultation since there is a specific request made by the primary care physician. This request can be in the form of a telephone call, written prescription, or other communication from the requesting physician to the consulting physician. The consulting physician in turn communicates the findings of the consultation to the requesting physician. This is most appropriately done in the form of a written communication back to the requesting physician. It is appropriate and acceptable for the consulting physician to initiate diagnostic and/or therapeutic interventions at the time of the initial consultation. If the documentation does not identify a request for a consultation by the treating physician, a report on the consultant's findings, and recommendations back to the treating physician, then the requirements for a consultation are not met.

If the patient in this vignette had seen the physiatrist directly, either without seeing the primary care physician or without a treating physician's request, then the encounter between the patient and the physiatrist would be an initial encounter and not a consultation.

In a scenario where a treating physician clearly identifies that he or she is referring a patient to another physician for that physician to take over the care of that patient (as opposed to a request for consultation), and the physician being asked to take over the care of the patient agrees to do so in advance, this would constitute a referral and the initial evaluation by the receiving physician would be an initial visit and not a consultation.

EXERCISE 2

Answer: A

99291 Critical care, evaluation and management of the critically ill or critically injured patient; first 30–74 minutes [by the emergency department physician]

99293 Initial inpatient pediatric critical care, 29 days through 24 months of age, per day, for the evaluation and management of a critically ill infant or young child [by the pediatrician]

Rationale for Code Selection

Pediatric Critical Care Services code **99293** is intended to be reported for the initial day of critical care provided in the *inpatient* setting. The critical care performed in the outpatient setting, such as the emergency department, should be reported with the hourly critical care codes (**99291–99292**), regardless of the age of the patient. Therefore, the emergency department physician would report only the critical care code **99291** for the first hour of critical care performed.

EXERCISE 3

Answer: 99392 Periodic comprehensive preventive medicine reevaluation and management of an individual including an age and gender appropriate history, examination, counseling/anticipatory guidance/risk factor reduction interventions, and the ordering of appropriate immunization(s), laboratory/diagnostic procedures, established patient; early childhood (age 1 through 4 years)

90700 Diptheria, tetanus toxoids, and acellular pertussis vaccine (DTaP), for intramuscular use

90471 Immunization administration (includes percutaneous, intradermal, subcutaneous, intramuscular and jet injections); one vaccine (single or combination vaccine/toxoid)

Rationale for Code Selection

As an uneventful well-child visit for an established patient between the ages of 1 and 4 years, the visit is reported with code **99392**. If the child were a new patient, the visit would be reported with code **99382**.

In addition, the DTaP immunization merits code **90700**. The corresponding administration code is **90471**.

EXERCISE 4

Answer: 99402 Preventive medicine counseling and/or risk factor reduction intervention(s) provided to an individual (separate procedure); approximately 30 minutes.

Rationale for Code Selection

The focus of this encounter is in providing counseling, specifically risk factor reduction and patient education, so an E/M code should be submitted. The patient's lack of a chief complaint or a symptom rules out the use of a standard office visit code. Instead, the appropriate code to submit is **99402**. According to CPT coding guidelines, preventive medicine codes **99401** to **99412** are to be used for services provided "at a separate encounter for the purpose of promoting health and preventing illness or injury" for patients without symptoms or established illness. These codes may be used to describe counseling, anticipatory guidance, or risk factor reduction interventions provided separately from or without a preventive service examination.

EXERCISE 5

Answer: 99285 Emergency department visit for the evaluation and management of a patient, which requires these three key components within the constraints imposed by the urgency of the patient's clinical condition and/or mental status

Rationale for Code Selection

While the patient's medical condition might appear to meet the criteria for critical care, the physician did not provide services for a sufficient length of time to be eligible to report Critical Care Services code **99291**. Code **99291** requires a minimum of 30 minutes of critical care services provision, in total, for the patient by the physician on any one date. Therefore, the appropriate emergency department (ED) E/M service should be reported.

It seems evident that the nature of the patient's presenting problem is consistent with code **99285**. While it is noted that the medical history and physical examination available and/or performed are insufficient to satisfy the criteria for the key components of code **99285**, the descriptor for code **99285** allows the criteria for the key components to be waived when appropriate (ie, "...within the constraints imposed by the urgency of the patient's clinical condition and/or mental status"). Such waiver of criteria for key components is allowable only with code **99285** in the ED E/M code set.

EXERCISE 6

Answer: Emergency Department Services code (**99281–99285**) appropriate to service performed and documented in medical record.

99291 Critical care, evaluation and management of the critically ill or critically injured patient; first 30–74 minutes.

93010 Electrocardiogram, routine ECG with at least 12 leads; interpretation and report only.

31500 Intubation, endotracheal, emergency procedure

92950 Cardiopulmonary resuscitation (eg, in cardiac arrest)

93010-76 Electrocardiogram, routine ECG with at least 12 leads; interpretation and report only

93042 Rhythm ECG, one to three leads; interpretation and report only

Rationale for Code Selection

Code **99291**: For most ED patients, critical care services can be reported in addition to other E/M services provided on the same date. The patient was critically ill for 80 minutes, during which time the attending ED physician was providing services. However, the time spent in separately reportable services performed during critical care (eg, codes **92950**, **31500**, **93010**, **93042**, etc) cannot be counted in determining the total physician-provided critical care service time. In this instance, code **92950** comprised 20 minutes. The performance of the other separately reportable services would consume some additional time, leaving a total assessable physician-provided critical care service time as the physician documented at 44 minutes.

Code **93010**: Since the ECG was performed in the hospital by hospital-employed (rather than physician-employed) staff using hospital-owned equipment, only the interpretation and report is reported by the physician.

Code **31500**: Endotracheal intubation is not included in the cardiopulmonary resuscitation service, which encompasses basic cardiopulmonary resuscitation activities only. The endotracheal intubation is also not included in critical care services and is therefore reported separately. However, the time spent in providing the endotracheal intubation service cannot be counted when the total physician-provided critical care service time is determined for coding purposes.

Code **92950**: Basic cardiopulmonary resuscitation consists of assessing the patient, opening the airway, restoring breathing (eg, mouth-to-mouth, bag valve mask), then restoring circulation (eg, closed-chest cardiac massage). In most instances, cardiopulmonary resuscitation is performed first, sometimes with continuation during advanced life support interventions (eg, drug therapy and defibrillation), that would be included by reporting the appropriate critical care service code(s). Also, if endotracheal intubation was performed, it would be appropriate to separately report code **31500**.

Code **93010-76**: ECG interpretation is not included in critical care or the cardiopulmonary resuscitation service. Since the ECG was performed in the hospital by hospital-employed (rather than physician-employed) staff using hospital-owned equipment, only the interpretation and report is reported by the physician. Also, because the ECG service (**93010**) was performed subsequent to the initial ECG service (**93010**) on the same date, for the same patient, by the same physician, this additional procedure may be identified by appending the modifier 76 (Repeat Procedure by Same Physician).

Code **93042**: Rhythm ECG is not included in critical care and in cardiopulmonary resuscitation. Since the rhythm ECG was performed in the hospital by hospital-employed (rather than physician-employed) staff using hospital-owned equipment, only the interpretation and report are reported by the physician.

EXERCISE 7

Answer: 99214 Office or other outpatient visit for the evaluation and management of an established patient, which requires at least two of these three key components:

- a detailed history;
- a detailed examination;
- medical decision making of moderate complexity.

99354 Prolonged physician service in the office or other outpatient setting requiring direct (face-to-face) patient contact beyond the usual service (eg, prolonged care and treatment of an acute asthmatic patient in an outpatient setting); first hour (List separately in addition to code for office or other outpatient Evaluation and Management service)

Rationale for Code Selection

Prolonged service codes are reported when the service for direct patient contact exceeds the usual time spent for the patient encounter. The code is reported in addition to the E/M code for the patient visit (consultation, new patient, or established patient). The basis for billing is time, and not history, physical examination, or medical decision making. Documentation of the reason for the prolonged service must be included in the record. In this case, the neurologist spent 75 minutes face-to-face with the patient, because of the extended amount of outside records and complexity of the case.

The base E/M code in this scenario is **99214**, which typically requires 25 minutes face-to-face with the patient. The Prolonged Services code **99354** is reported for the first hour of prolonged outpatient service beyond the E/M service typical time. An hour is defined as 31 to 74 minutes. In this case, the face-to-face time was 25 plus 50 minutes. Thus, codes **99214** and **99354** are reported. If the physician spent 90 minutes face-to-face, then the appropriate coding would be **99214** plus Prolonged Services codes **99354** and **99355** once each. The code **99355** is for each additional half-hour beyond the 74-minute limit defined for code **99354**.

EXERCISE 8

Answer: 99291 Critical care, evaluation and management of the critically ill or critically injured patient; first 30–74 minutes (Report code **99291** once.)

99292 Critical care, evaluation and management of the critically ill or critically injured patient; each additional 30 minutes (Report code **99292** three times.)

Rationale for Code Selection

Critical care codes **99291** and **99292** are used to report the total duration of time spent by a physician providing critical care services to a critically ill or critically injured patient, even if the time spent by the physician on that date is not continuous. For any given period of time spent providing critical care services, the physician must devote full attention to the patient and, therefore, cannot provide services to any other patient during the same period. In this scenario, the neurologist spent two and one-half hours (150 minutes) providing critical care services on the same date. Therefore, code **99291** should be reported once, and code **99292** should be reported three times.

Chapter 2

Anesthesia Answers

EXERCISE 1

Answer: 00540 Anesthesia for thoracotomy procedures involving lungs, pleura, diaphragm, and mediastinum (including surgical thoracoscopy); not otherwise specified

62318-59 Injection, including catheter placement, continuous infusion or intermittent bolus, not including neurolytic substances, with or without contrast (for either localization or epidurography), of diagnostic or therapeutic substance(s) (including anesthetic, antispasmodic, opioid, steroid, other solution), epidural or subarachnoid; cervical or thoracic

Rationale for Code Selection

If the catheter is retained for control of postoperative pain, report the daily management for subsequent day(s) with code **01996** (daily hospital management of epidural or subarachnoid continuous drug administration).

> **CODING TIP**
>
> If the block or epidural was placed to provide anesthesia for the procedure, report only the appropriate anesthesia code (**00100–01999**). The pain procedure would not be a separately reportable service in that instance.

> **CODING TIP**
>
> Code **01996** applies only to epidural or subarachnoid drug administration and is not applicable to peripheral nerve blocks.

EXERCISE 2

Answer: 01400 Anesthesia for open or surgical arthroscopic procedures on knee joint; not otherwise specified

64447-59 Injection, anesthetic agent; femoral nerve, single

Rationale for Code Selection

Code **01400** is the appropriate anesthesia code as it describes an open or an arthroscopic surgical procedure. Since the case is done with the patient under general anesthesia, the femoral nerve injection is separately reportable.

Code **64447-59** is reported for the femoral nerve block, performed by the anesthesiologist for postoperative pain control. Per anesthesia guidelines, oxygen saturation and intravenous access are included in the anesthesia codes and are not reported separately.

> **CODING TIP**
>
> The combination of **01967** and **+01968** is not the same as code **01961**. Code **01961**—Anesthesia for cesarean delivery only—is used when the patient did not receive a labor epidural and describes regional or general anesthesia.

EXERCISE 3

Answer: 01967 Neuraxial labor analgesia/anesthesia for planned vaginal delivery (this includes any repeat subarachnoid needle placement and drug injection and/or any necessary replacement of an epidural catheter during labor)

+01968 Anesthesia for cesarean delivery following neuraxial labor analgesia/anesthesia

Postoperative Pain Management: If catheter is retained, code **01996** is reported; if catheter is removed, an E/M code is reported.

Rationale for Code Selection

When a patient receives a labor epidural and goes on to deliver vaginally, code **01967** is reported. If that labor ends with a cesarean section, both **01967** and the add-on code **01968** are reported.

EXERCISE 4

Answer:	**01173**	Anesthesia for open repair of fracture disruption of pelvis or column fracture involving acetabulum
	36620	Arterial catheterization or cannulation for sampling, monitoring or transfusion (separate procedure); percutaneous
	36556	Insertion of non-tunneled centrally inserted central venous catheter; age 5 years or older

Rationale for Code Selection

Monitoring of invasive lines is included in an anesthesia service, but their *placement* is not.

Insertion of Non-Tunneled Centrally Inserted Central Venous Catheter

36556

During placement of a central venous catheter, a short tract is developed as the catheter is advanced from the skin entry site to the point of venous cannulation. The catheter tip must reside in the subclavian, innominate or iliac veins, the inferior vena cava/superior vena cava, or right atrium, to be considered a "central venous" catheter.

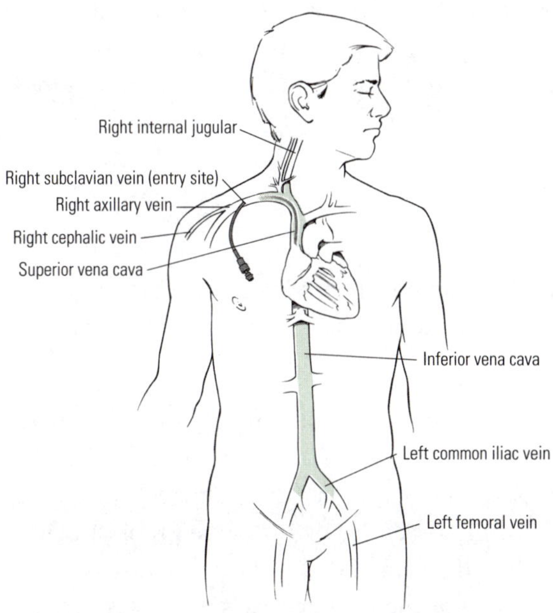

Chapter 3

Surgery Answers

Integumentary System

EXERCISE 1

Answer: False

Rationale for Code Selection

It would *not* be appropriate to report two excision of lesion codes if an additional excision is performed at the same surgical session for complete tumor removal. Instead, only one code should be reported on the basis of the final widest excised diameter.

EXERCISE 2

Answer: B Report two codes for each excision.

Rationale for Code Selection

As indicated in the Excision—Malignant Lesions guidelines, each malignant lesion excised should be reported separately. The appropriate method of reporting excision of a malignant lesion from the left arm with excised diameter of 1.5 cm and excision of a malignant lesion from the right arm with excised diameter of 2.0 cm is with code **11602**, Excision, malignant lesion including margins, trunk, arms, or legs; excised diameter 1.1 to 2.0 cm, reported two times. Modifier 59, Distinct Procedural Service, should be appended to the second code to indicate that a distinct procedure was performed on a different anatomic site.

EXERCISE 3

Answer: A

11601-58 Excision, malignant lesion including margins, trunk, arms, or legs; excised diameter 0.6 cm to 1.0 cm

Rationale for Code Selection

Re-excision procedures performed to widen margins at subsequent operative sessions should be reported by using the appropriate code identifying the size, location, and type of excision performed during the reexcision. Modifier 58, Staged or Related Procedure or Service by the Same Physician During the Postoperative Period, should be appended if the procedure is performed during the postoperative period of the primary excision procedure. Therefore, code **11601**, Excision, malignant lesion including margins, trunk, arms, or legs; excised diameter 0.6 to 1.0 cm, should be reported for the reexcision with modifier 58 appended.

EXERCISE 4

Answer: C — The measurement of the greatest clinical diameter of apparent lesion plus the margins required for complete excision.

Rationale for Code Selection

As stated in the revised guidelines for the codes for excision of lesions, "Code selection is determined by measuring the greatest clinical diameter of the apparent lesion plus that margin required for complete excision." If, for example, a benign lesion of the trunk measures 1.0 cm and the margins required to adequately excise the lesion are 0.5 cm on both sides, then the size of the lesion is added to the margins on either side (1.0 cm + 0.5 cm + 0.5 cm = 2.0 cm). In this case, code **11402**, Excision, benign lesion including margins, except skin tag (unless listed elsewhere), trunk, arms, or legs; excised diameter 1.1 to 2.0 cm, should be reported to reflect the benign lesion and necessary margin excised from the trunk.

EXERCISE 5

Answer: False

Rationale for Code Selection

As indicated in the descriptor of code **17304** Chemosurgery (Mohs micrographic technique), including removal of all gross tumor, surgical excision of tissue specimens, mapping, color coding of specimens, microscopic examination of specimens by the surgeon, and complete histopathologic preparation including the first routine stain (eg, hematoxylin and eosin, toluidine blue); first stage, fresh tissue technique, up to 5 specimens, the complete histopathologic preparation includes the routine tissue staining. However, special stains are separately reportable. This is referenced in the parenthetical note following code **17304**.

EXERCISE 6

Answer: B

11623 Excision, malignant lesion including margins, scalp, neck, hands, feet, genitalia; excised diameter 2.1 to 3.0 cm

15120 Split graft, face scalp, eyelids, mouth, neck, ears, orbits, genitalia, hands, feet and/or multiple digits; first 100 sq cm or less, or one percent of body area of infants and children (except **15050**)

Rationale for Code Selection

When working with both millimeters (mm) and centimeters (cm), it is important to convert to centimeters to accurately add and report the excised diameter. In this scenario, 5 mm = 0.5 cm or a total of 1.0 cm for the entire margin. Therefore, 1.8 cm for the lesion plus 1.0 cm for the entire margin equals 2.8 cm. Code selection is determined by measuring the greatest clinical diameter of the lesion, plus that margin required for complete excision. For a split-thickness skin graft, procedures are coded by the size of this graft and the location of the recipient site. In this scenario, it is the hand.

EXERCISE 7

Answer: A

> **11301** Shaving of epidermal or dermal lesion, single lesion, trunk, arms or legs; lesion diameter 0.6 to 1.0 cm

Rationale for Code Selection

The presenting lesion was consistent with that of an inflamed nevus. Such lesions may be removed in a variety of ways, including excision with linear repair as well as shave removal of only the elevated component subject to irritation. The choice between the two techniques is made generally by the physician and patient and may be determined in part by efforts to minimize scarring, especially when the lesion is not suspected to be malignant. In this instance, the lesion does not require wide margins for removal. Therefore, assuming 1-mm margins at the base of the lesion (total margin = 2 mm), the shave removal diameter of the lesion would be 9 mm (7 mm + 2 mm = 9 mm = 0.9 cm).

EXERCISE 8

Answer A: False
Answer B: True

Rationale for Code Selection

New introductory language under the subheading Biopsy was added to clarify accurate reporting of biopsy procedures in the skin, subcutaneous tissue, and/or mucous membrane:

> During certain surgical procedures in the integumentary system, such as excision, destruction, or shave removals, the removed tissue is often submitted for pathologic examination. The obtaining of tissue for pathology during the course of these procedures is a routine component of such procedures. This obtaining of tissue is not considered a separate biopsy procedure and is not separately reported. The use of a biopsy procedure code (eg, **11100**, **11101**) indicates that the procedure to obtain tissue for pathologic examination was performed independently, or was unrelated or distinct from other procedures/services provided at that time. Such biopsies are not considered components of other procedures when performed on different lesions or different sites on the same date, and are to be reported separately.

In Exercise 8A, the code is based on just the excised diameter. The intention of the physician was to excise the mole and send it to pathology to determine the possible need for further surgery. The submission of the lesion to pathology was a routine pathological examination, as indicated by the new introductory language stated previously.

In Exercise 8B, however, both codes are reported because the punch biopsy is a separate procedure. Since the punch biopsy was performed to obtain tissue for pathological examination and was unrelated to the excision of the basal cell carcinoma excision, code **11100** is separately reported with modifier 59 appended to identify that it was a distinct procedural service.

EXERCISE 9

Answer: 11750 Excision of nail and nail matrix, partial or complete (eg, ingrown or deformed nail) for permanent removal

Rationale for Code Selection

Code **11750** is reported for the removal of nail and nail matrix, whether it is partial or complete.

EXERCISE 10

Answer: 15000 Surgical preparation or creation of recipient site by excision of open wounds, burn eschar, or scar (including subcutaneous tissues); first 100 sq cm or one percent of body area of infants and children

15342 Application of bilaminate skin substitute/neodermis; 25 sq cm

Rationale for Code Selection

It is important to remember that a separate code is reported for the surgical preparation of the recipient site. There are separate codes for various types of skin grafts and skin substitute. In this scenario, bilaminate skin substitute was applied.

Musculoskeletal System

EXERCISE 1

Answer: 20610 Arthrocentesis, aspiration and/or injection; major joint or bursa (eg, shoulder, hip, knee joint, subacromial bursa)

EXERCISE 2

Answer: 20551 Injection(s); single tendon origin/insertion

EXERCISE 3

Answer: 28296 Correction, hallux valgus (bunion), with or without sesamoidectomy; with metatarsal osteotomy (eg, Mitchell, Chevron, or concentric type procedures)

28285-59 Correction, hammertoe (eg, interphalangeal fusion, partial or total phalangectomy)

Rationale for Code Selection

Modifier 59 is appended to indicate that the correction of the hammertoe is identified as a distinct procedural service from the bunionetomy.

EXERCISE 4

Answer: 63075 Diskectomy, anterior, with decompression of spinal cord and/or nerve root(s), including osteophytectomy; cervical, single interspace [for the anterior cervical diskectomy performed at C5-C6]

22554-51	Arthrodesis, anterior interbody technique, including minimal diskectomy to prepare interspace (other than for decompression); cervical below C2 [for the anterior cervical arthrodesis performed at C5-C6]
20931	Allograft for spine surgery only; structural [for the preparation and impaction of the allograft into the interspace at C5-C6]
22845	Anterior instrumentation; 2 to 3 vertebral segments [for the anterior cervical plate instrumentation placed at C5-C6]

Rationale for Code Selection

There are some appropriate procedural circumstances when codes **22554** and **63075** may be reported together. For example, if the surgeon is excising the disk and preparing the vertebral end plates for acceptance of the graft, then this is considered part of the arthrodesis and code **63075** would not be additionally reported. However, if neural elements, dura, and/or nerve roots are decompressed, then code **63075** may be reported in addition to code **22554**. Typically, the operative report should specifically identify decompression of neural elements.

Therefore, on the basis of the specific information presented in this operative case, the decompression procedure **63075** would be reported in addition to code **22554** (with modifier 51 appended to reflect multiple procedures).

Anterior Approach for Cervical Fusion

22554

An example of an exposure technique used to reach anterior cervical vertebrae for spinal procedures (eg, diskectomy, arthrodesis, spinal instrumentation).

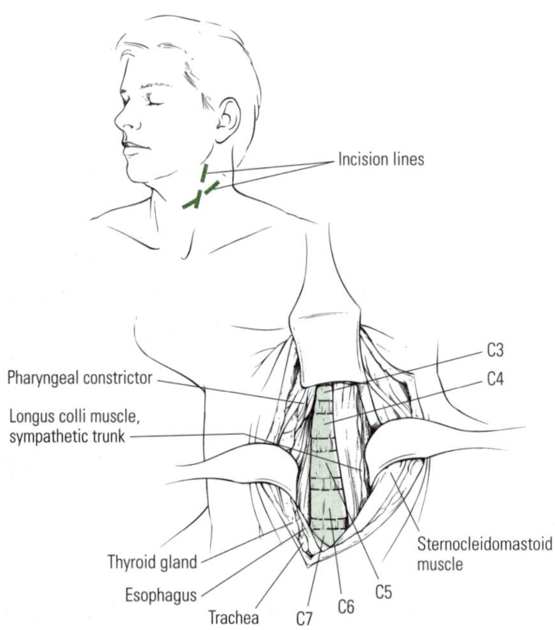

It is important to note that the operating microscope code **69990** Microsurgical techniques, requiring use of operating microscope (List separately in addition to code for primary procedure), should *not* be reported since use of the operating microscope is an inclusive component of code **63075**.

Additionally, when multiple procedures other than E/M services are performed at the same session by the same provider, the primary procedure or service is reported, and the additional procedure(s) or service(s) is identified by appending modifier 51, Multiple Procedures, to the additional procedure or service code(s).

Historically, payers and providers have used the modifier 51 in varying ways. To alleviate confusion about the intent of the modifier, the definition includes language to indicate that it is not appended to add-on codes, as listed in Appendix D of the CPT codebook, E/M codes, or codes designated as modifier 51 exempt, as listed in Appendix E of the CPT codebook.

On the basis of the above information, modifier 51 is not appended to codes **20931** and **22845**, as they are designated modifier 51 exempt.

EXERCISE 5

Answer: 29075 Application, cast; elbow to finger (short arm)

Rationale for Code Selection

Appropriate level of E/M code from the Emergency Department Services codes (**99281–99285**) provided the appropriate key components are met. The emergency department physician is responsible only for the initial service of casting the fractured arm. The physician will not perform, and does not expect to perform, any restorative treatment. In addition, the physician will not assume all subsequent fracture care and has instructed the patient to follow up with an orthopedic physician.

EXERCISE 6

Answer: 27752 Closed treatment of tibial shaft fracture (with or without fibular fracture); with manipulation, with or without skeletal traction [by the orthopedic surgeon]

Appropriate level E/M code from the Consultation codes (**99241–99245**) provided the appropriate key components are met [by the orthopedic surgeon].

Rationale for Code Selection

In this scenario, it is important to consider that the orthopedic surgeon provided a restorative treatment and is responsible for subsequent fracture care under the surgical package. The cast application cannot be reported separately because the services described in code **27752** include the first cast.

EXERCISE 7

Answer: 29826 Arthroscopy, shoulder, surgical; decompression of subacromial space with partial acromioplasty, with or without coracoacromial release

29822-51 Arthroscopy, shoulder, surgical; debridement, limited

Rationale for Code Selection

Code **29826** is reported for the surgical arthroscopy of the shoulder with partial acromioplasty, arch decompression, excision of bursal tissue, and release of the coracoacromial ligament. Code **29822** is reported for the limited debridement of the labral and rotator cuff tissues. This arthroscopic procedure involves exposing the subacromial space, bursectomy, debridement, detaching the coracoacromial ligament, and removing the undersurface of the acromion. When subacromial decompression is performed, a flat undersurface of the acromion and acromioclavicular joint is produced, which enlarges the supraspinatus outlet and prevents impingement.

It would not be appropriate to report code **29805**, Arthroscopy, shoulder, diagnostic, with or without synovial biopsy (separate procedure), in addition to the surgical arthroscopy code **29826** or **29822**, since **29805** is designated as a "separate procedure." Codes designated as separate procedures may not be additionally reported when the procedure or service is performed as an integral component of another procedure or service. As with all arthroscopic procedures in the CPT codebook, a diagnostic arthroscopy is considered to be an inclusive component of a surgical arthroscopy and would not be reported separately.

The partial acromioplasty, arch decompression, excision of bursal tissue, and release of the coracoacromial ligament are also not be reported separately, as these are considered to be inclusive components of code **29826**.

Modifier 51 is appended to code **29822** to indicate that it is a multiple procedure, secondary to code **29826**. When multiple procedures or services are performed at the same session by the same provider, the primary procedure would be reported as listed in the CPT codebook. The additional procedure(s) or service(s) may be identified by appending the modifier 51, Multiple Procedures, to the additional procedure or service code(s).

EXERCISE 8

Answer: 29889 Arthroscopically aided posterior cruciate ligament repair/augmentation or reconstruction

Rationale for Code Selection

Arthroscopically aided posterior cruciate ligament repair, augmentation, or reconstruction should not be reported with codes **27427–27429**, as these codes are "open" surgical procedures and should not be used to report this procedure by the arthroscopic approach.

Respiratory System

EXERCISE 1

Answer: 31628 Bronchoscopy, rigid or flexible, with or without fluoroscopic guidance; with transbronchial lung biopsy(s), single lobe

Rationale for Code Selection

Code **31628** is reported for the transbronchial biopsy in the right lower lobe. Even though three to six biopsies were obtained, code **31628** is reported only once, as the descriptors states *biopsy(s)*, which indicates that this code is reported for one or multiple transbronchial biopsies. Also, fluoroscopic guidance is not reported separately since it is included in this procedure.

EXERCISE 2

Answer: 30420 Rhinoplasty, primary; including major septal repair

31254-50-51 Nasal/sinus endoscopy, surgical; with ethmoidectomy, partial (anterior)

31256-50-51 Nasal/sinus endoscopy, surgical, with maxillary antrostomy

Modifier 50 Bilateral Procedure: Unless otherwise identified in the listings, bilateral procedures that are performed at the same operative session should be identified by adding modifier 50 to the appropriate five-digit code.

Modifier 51 Multiple Procedures: When multiple procedures or services are performed at the same session by the same provider, the primary procedure would be reported as listed in the CPT codebook. The additional procedure(s) or service(s) may be identified by appending Modifier 51, Multiple Procedures, to the additional procedure or service code(s).

Rationale for Code Selection

Code **30420** is reported for the deviated portion of the septum. Code **31254** is reported for the nasal/sinus endoscopy with bilateral partial ethmoidectomies. Modifier 50 should be appended to indicate that this procedure was performed on both sides. Modifier 51 should be appended to indicate multiple procedures. Code **31256** is reported to reflect the performance of bilateral maxillary antrostomies. Modifier 50 should be appended to indicate that this procedure was performed on both sides. Modifier 51 should be appended to indicate multiple procedures. It is important to note that the resection of the middle turbinate on the right side is not reported, even though the patient did have maxillary antrostomies performed additionally. The middle turbinate is anatomically a part of the ethmoid bone. Typically, if the middle turbinate is removed when an endoscopic ethmoidectomy or polypectomy is performed, the removal of the middle turbinate is not additionally reported, as it is usually considered a part of the approach. However, if the inferior turbinate was removed in addition to the ethmoidectomy, then the removal of the inferior turbinate would be reported.

Cardiovascular System

EXERCISE 1

Answer: True

Rationale for Code Selection

According to CPT coding guidelines, if removal and replacement procedures are performed, then *both* procedures are reported separately.

EXERCISE 2

Answer: **33208** Insertion of permanent pacemaker with transvenous electrode(s); atrial and ventricular

33233 Removal of permanent pacemaker pulse generator

33235 Removal of transvenous pacemaker electrode(s); dual lead system

Rationale for Code Selection

A dual-chamber pacemaker system involves the insertion of electrodes into both the atrium and the right ventricle that are then connected to a pulse generator capable of pacing and sensing both the atrium and the ventricle. If removal and replacement procedures are performed, then both procedures are reported separately. Code **33208** is reported for the insertion of the permanent pacemaker and electrodes in the atrium and ventricle. Codes **33233** and **33235** are reported for the removal of the pulse generator (battery) and transvenous electrodes, dual lead system.

EXERCISE 3

Answer: **35600** Harvest of upper extremity artery, one segment, for coronary artery bypass procedure

Rationale for Code Selection

Code **35600** is intended to report the harvest of an upper extremity artery for use in coronary artery bypass grafting (CABG). This includes the procurement, implantation, and management of the free radial artery graft. Use of other arteries listed in the Coronary Artery Bypass Graft guidelines are included within the CABG procedure.

Harvest of Upper Extremity Artery
35600

Open procurement of a radial artery to secure conduit for construction of a coronary artery bypass graft.

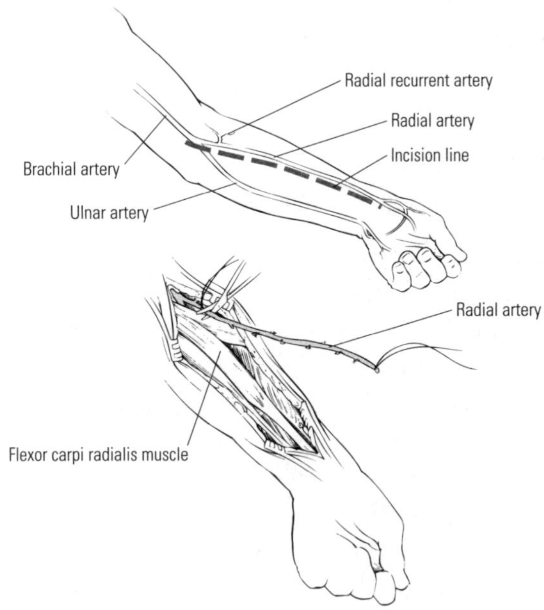

EXERCISE 4

Answer: False

Rationale for Code Selection

Procurement of the upper extremity vein is not included when a CABG or lower extremity bypass procedure is reported. Code **35500** is separately reported in addition to the grafting procedure for the harvest of a single vein segment for use in a lower extremity bypass or CABG procedure.

EXERCISE 5

Answer: **33533** Coronary artery bypass, using arterial graft(s); single arterial graft

33517 Coronary artery bypass, using venous graft(s) and arterial graft(s); single vein graft (List separately in addition to code for arterial graft)

33530 Reoperation, coronary artery bypass procedure or valve procedure, more than one month after original operation (List separately in addition to code for primary procedure)

Rationale for Code Selection

Code **33533** is reported for the single arterial graft, left internal mammary artery to left anterior descending artery. Code **33517** is reported for the single venous graft, saphenous vein graft to the right coronary artery. Since this was a reoperation, with the original CABG being performed two years previously, code **33530** is reported for the reoperation. Code **33530** is reported to reflect the increased difficulty associated with the coronary artery bypass reoperation.

Digestive System

EXERCISE 1

Answer: 45380 Colonoscopy, flexible proximal to splenic flexure, with biopsy, single or multiple

Rationale for Code Selection

CPT code **45380** does not describe a specific technique. The terminology is accepted and understood by endoscopists to mean the use of a forceps to grasp and remove a small piece of tissue without the application of cautery. Colonoscopy reports may describe the biopsy of a lesion or polyp by using a cold forceps or may describe the biopsy without mentioning the specific device. The biopsy may be from an obvious lesion too large to remove, from a suspicious area of abnormal mucosa, or from a lesion or polyp *so small* that it can be completely removed in the performance of the biopsy, which is often demonstrated with the cold biopsy forceps technique. The technique is the same and the service is reported with code **45380** regardless of the final histology of the piece of tissue obtained for analysis. Colonoscopy with removal by snare technique, **45385**, should *not* be used for a report describing the removal of a small polyp by "biopsy" or "cold forceps" technique.

EXERCISE 2

Answer: 45385 Colonoscopy, flexible, proximal to splenic flexure; with removal of tumor(s), polyp(s), or other lesion(s) by snare technique

Rationale for Code Selection

Code **45385** is reported for the snare removal of the polyp in its entirety.

EXERCISE 3

Answer: 45380-22 Colonoscopy, flexible, proximal to splenic flexure; with biopsy, single or multiple [with unusual procedure modifier]

Rationale for Code Selection

Although the CPT code descriptor says "single or multiple" biopsies, the unusual number of biopsies required for ulcerative colitis surveillance for dysplasia requires an inordinate amount of time over that of the standard colonoscopy with biopsies. Therefore, it would be appropriate for modifier 22 to be appended to the standard code and the claim to be submitted for paper review.

CODING TIP

When modifier 22 is used, it is important to document the number of biopsies as well as the amount of time spent during the procedure as compared to the more typical procedure to allow for appropriate reimbursement for the additional work required.

EXERCISE 4

Answer: 43245 Upper gastrointestinal endoscopy including esophagus, stomach, and either the duodenum and/or jejunum as appropriate; with dilation of gastric outlet for obstruction (eg, balloon, guide wire, bougie)

43239-51 Upper gastrointestinal endoscopy including esophagus, stomach, and either the duodenum and/or jejunum as appropriate; with biopsy, single or multiple

Rationale for Code Selection

Code **43239** is reported for the biopsies of the erosions in the stomach. Code **43245** is reported for the "through-the-scope" balloon dilation of the anastomosis.

EXERCISE 5

Answer: 43262 Endoscopic retrograde cholangiopancreatography (ERCP); with sphincterotomy/papillotomy.

43268-51 Endoscopic retrograde cholangiopancreatography (ERCP); with endoscopic retrograde insertion of tube or stent into bile or pancreatic duct

Rationale for Code Selection

Code **43262** is reported for ERCP with sphincterotomy in the proximal bile duct. If a stand-alone procedure, ERCP with brushings obtained from the bile duct stricture is reported with code **43260**; however, this is incorporated into **43262** and not reported separately. Code **43268** is reported for the stent placement across the stricture.

EXERCISE 6

Answer: 45380 Colonoscopy, flexible, proximal to splenic flexure; with biopsy, single or multiple

Rationale for Code Selection

Though multiple biopsies were taken, the code can only be reported once.

Urinary System

EXERCISE 1

Answer: 50590 Lithotripsy, extracorporeal shock wave

52332-51 Cystourethroscopy, with insertion of indwelling ureteral stent (eg, Gibbons or double-J type)

76000-26 Fluoroscopy (separate procedure), up to one hour physician time, other than **71023** or **71034** (eg, cardiac fluoroscopy)

CODING TIP

Modifier 51 has four applications, namely, to identify:

- Multiple medical procedures performed at the same session by the same provider
- Multiple, related operative procedures performed at the same session by the same provider
- Operative procedures performed in combination, at the same operative session, by the same provider, whether through the same or another incision or involving the same or different anatomy
- A combination of medical and operative procedures at the same session by the same provider

If the physician is performing more than one surgical procedure (combination, multiple procedures) on the same day or same session, the physician determines the primary procedure and then appends modifier 51 to the secondary procedures. The procedure that identifies the major or most resource-intensive procedure is listed first on the claim form, followed by the secondary procedure(s).

Rationale for Code Selection

CPT code **50590** is used to describe the fragmentation of stone by use of ultrasonic waves. An additional procedure is performed to insert ureteral stents to allow the stone fragments to pass down the ureter and out through the bladder. Since the physician used fluoroscopy with the hospital's equipment, the physician can report only the professional component, ie, supervision and interpretation of the test, so modifier 26 is appended to the fluoroscopy code. Modifier 51 is attached to the stent procedure **52332** to indicate that multiple procedures were performed.

EXERCISE 2

Answer:	**52353-78**	**Cystourethroscopy, with ureteroscopy and/or pyeloscopy; with lithotripsy (ureteral catheterization is included)**
	52332-59-78	Cystourethroscopy, with insertion of indwelling ureteral stent (eg, Gibbons or double-J type)
	52353-79	Cystourethroscopy, with ureteroscopy and/or pyeloscopy; with lithotripsy (ureteral catheterization is included)
	52332-59-79	Cystourethroscopy, with insertion of indwelling ureteral stent (eg, Gibbons or double-J type)
	76000-26	Fluoroscopy (separate procedure), up to one hour physician time, other than **71023** or **71034** (eg, cardiac fluoroscopy)
	74420-26	Urography, retrograde, with or without KUB

Rationale for Code Selection

The procedures performed on this patient represent a common scenario a urologist must face when treating renal or ureteral calculi. The use of radiological equipment to locate the stone and other therapies for treatment and removal are necessary. Since the patient has stones on both sides of the body and is under anesthesia, the physician must decide whether treatment is necessary for all stones involved at one time. In this case, the urologist has chosen to try to take care of all stones in this treatment setting. There are also complications from the intial extracorporeal shock wave lithotripsy because of large stone fragments blocking the ureter. The use of modifier 59 shows that some of the procedures were performed on a different (in this case opposite) body area, and the use of modifier 78 indicates that the patient was returned to the operating room for a procedure related to the initial extracorporeal shock wave lithotripsy during the postoperative period. The use of modifier 79, Unrelated Procedure or Service by the Same Physician During the Postoperative Period, was appended to the procedures (ureteroscopy with laser lithotripsy and stent insertion) used to treat the left-sided stones.

EXERCISE 3

Answer: 52647 Non-contact laser coagulation of prostate, including control of postoperative bleeding, complete (vasectomy, meatotomy, cystourethroscopy, urethral calibration and/or dilation, and internal urethrotomy are included)

EXERCISE 4

Answer: 52648 Contact laser vaporization with or without transurethral resection of prostate, including control of postoperative bleeding, complete (vasectomy, meatotomy, cystourethroscopy, urethral calibration and/or dilation, and internal urethrotomy are included)

Contact Laser Vaporization of Prostate

52648

A laser is used to vaporize the prostate.

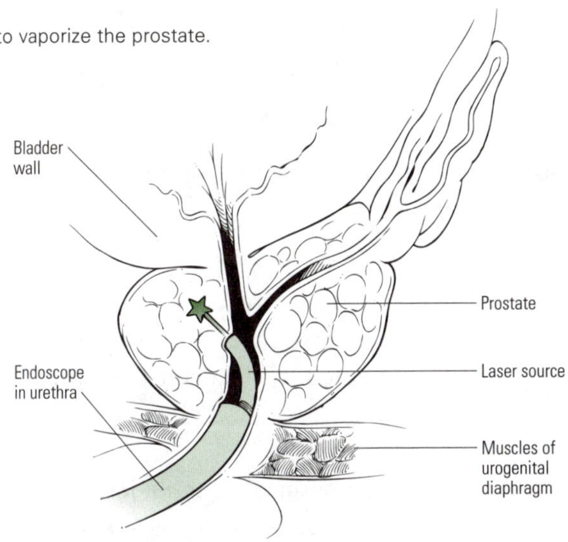

Female Genital System

EXERCISE 1

Answer: 57456 Colposcopy of the cervix including upper/adjacent vagina; with endocervical curettage

56821-51 Colposcopy of the vulva; with biopsy(s)

Rationale for Code Selection

Code **56821** describes endoscopic examination, magnification, and biopsy of the vulva to evaluate for viral lesions, neoplasia, or malignancy. If multiple biopsies are performed on the vulva during the same session, then code **56821** should be reported only one time, as indicated by the optional plural form of biopsy(s). Modifier 51 is appended to indicate that this is an additional biopsy.

EXERCISE 2

Answer: 58760-50 Fimbrioplasty

Rationale for Code Selection

Since this was an open procedure, code **58760** was selected. Modifier 50, Bilateral Procedure, is appended to indicate that the fimbrioplasty was performed on both the right and left sides. Chromotubation is considered an inherent part of this procedure and is not reported separately.

EXERCISE 3

Answer: 58180 Supracervical abdominal hysterectomy (subtotal hysterectomy), with or without removal of tube(s), with or without removal of ovary(s)

57268-59 Repair of enterocele, vaginal approach (separate procedure)

EXERCISE 4

Answer: 58550 Laparoscopy, surgical, with vaginal hysterectomy, for uterus 250 grams or less

51990-51 Laparoscopy, surgical; urethral suspension for stress incontinence

Rationale for Code Selection

Since the uterus weighed less than 250 grams, code **58550** was selected. Since the hysterectomy codes are differentiated by uterine weight, it is important that the uterine weight be documented in the medical record.

EXERCISE 5

Answer: 58662 Laparoscopy, surgical; with fulguration or excision of lesions of the ovary, pelvic viscera, or peritoneal surface by any method

58558-51 Hysteroscopy, surgical; with sampling (biopsy) of endometrium and/or polypectomy, with or without dilation and curettage (D & C)

Maternity Care and Delivery

EXERCISE 1

Answer: 59515 Cesarean delivery only; including postpartum care

59426 Antepartum care only; 7 or more visits

Rationale for Code Selection

Code **59515** is reported by the obstetrician, as this physician provided the cesarean delivery and postpartum care services. Code **59426** is reported by the family physician, as this physician provided only 12 antepartum visits.

Nervous System

EXERCISE 1

Answer: **61793** Stereotactic radiosurgery (particle beam, gamma ray or linear accelerator), one or more sessions

61793-59 Stereotactic radiosurgery (particle beam, gamma ray or linear accelerator), one or more sessions

Rationale for Code Selection

Code **61793** may be reported twice, with either modifier 59, Distinct Procedural Service, or modifier 51, Multiple Procedures, appended to the second code (depending upon payer requirements). Code **61793** is valued for a single metastatic lesion. There is significantly more physician work involved for radiosurgical planning and treatment when more than one lesion is treated during a single operative session.

EXERCISE 2

Answer: False

Rationale for Code Selection

The codes for destruction by neurolytic agent, paraverebral facet joint nerve (**64622–64627**), are considered unilateral procedures. When both right-side and left-side injections are performed, the bilateral procedure modifier 50 is appended to the appropriate code (**64622-50**).

EXERCISE 3

Answer: **64612** Chemodenervation of muscle(s); muscle(s) innervated by facial nerve (eg, for blepharospasm, hemifacial spasm)

Rationale for Code Selection

Codes **64612–64614** are reported once, even though multiple injections are performed in sites along a particular muscle (several muscles are typically injected).

Eye and Ocular Adnexa

EXERCISE 1

Answer: **66170** Fistulization of sclera for glaucoma; trabeculectomy ab externo in absence of previous surgery

Rationale for Code Selection

CPT code selection is based on patient clinical history. Proper code selection is determined by checking the patient's history, progress, and/or consultation notes for the presence or absence of previous surgery, trauma, or scarring of the operated-on eye. Previous ocular surgery can result in scarring, distortion, or elimination of ocular surgical landmarks. For a patient who has not had previous ocular surgery on the operated-on eye, code **66170** is reported.

Code **66172** is reported for a patient who has scarring from previous ocular surgery or trauma to the operated-on eye.

Laterality of the operated-on eye is always indicated by using HCPCS level II modifier LT or RT, as appropriate.

Use of an operating microscope is not reported separately, as it is included in the procedure code.

EXERCISE 2

Answer: B

67145 Prophylaxis of retinal detachment (eg, retinal break, lattice degeneration) without drainage, one or more sessions; photocoagulation (laser or xenon arc)

Rationale for Code Selection

The guidelines above code **67145** explain that the codes that follow them are repetitive services. The guidelines also state that the services are often performed in multiple sessions or groups of sessions, and therefore the descriptors include all sessions in a defined treatment period. Code **67145** is reported only once for the three sessions.

EXERCISE 3

Answer: **66984-53** Extracapsular cataract removal with insertion of intraocular lens prosthesis (one stage procedure), manual or mechanical technique (eg, irrigation and aspiration or phacoemulsification)

Rationale for Code Selection

Code **66984** is reported for the extracapsular cataract procedure. A popular type of extracapsular cataract extraction in the last few years has been phacoemulsification. If an intraocular lens is implanted after phacoemulsification, CPT code **66984** is the appropriate code to report.

The CPT codes for reporting extracapsular surgery are **66840**, **66850**, **66852**, **66940**, **66982**, and **66984**. Extracapsular cataract surgery is performed by expressing the entire lens or by fragmenting and aspiration, called *phacofragmentation*. The latter method uses either a vitrectomy/cutting instrument, which chops the lens into fragments, or an ultrasonic instrument (eg, phacoemulsification), which shatters the lens into fragments with ultrasonic energy. The fragments are then aspirated by the instrument. With each technique, the cataract is removed in a piecemeal fashion and a portion of the lens, the posterior capsule, is usually left behind.

Modifier 53, Discontinued Procedure, is appended to indicate that the cataract procedure was in fact begun and partially completed, but that extenuating circumstances prevented its completion. The descriptor for modifier 53, Discontinued Procedure, states: “Under certain circumstances, the physician may elect to terminate a surgical or diagnostic procedure. Due to extenuating circumstances or those that threaten the well being of the patient, it may be necessary to indicate that a surgical or diagnostic procedure was started but discontinued. . . . This modifier is not used to report the elective cancellation of a procedure prior to the patient's anesthesia induction and/or surgical preparation in the operating suite."

Modifier 53 differs from 52 (which describes a procedure that was reduced at the physician's discretion) in that a patient's life-threatening condition precipitates the terminated procedure.

Chapter 4

Radiology Answers

EXERCISES 1, 2, 3

Answer: (Exercise 1) **23350** Injection procedure for shoulder arthrography or enhanced CT/MRI shoulder arthrography

(Exercise 2) **73040** Radiologic examination, shoulder, arthrography, radiological supervision and interpretation

(Exercise 3) **73222** Magnetic resonance (eg, proton) imaging, any joint of upper extremity; with contrast material(s)

Rationale for Code Selection

Although a combined radiographic and MR study was performed, only one injection procedure was involved; therefore, **23350** is reported only once. The descriptor for the injection procedure (**23350**) includes all types of shoulder arthrographic exams, regardless of the imaging modality used (ie, radiographic, CT, or MR).

Since a radiographic arthrography procedure was performed in addition to MR arthrography, it is not appropriate to report the fluoroscopic guidance. Fluoroscopic guidance for needle placement, contrast injection, and any spot filming is included in the *radiographic* arthrography supervision and interpretation codes. In the scenario listed above, fluoroscopic guidance is included in code **73040**.

There are three codes to describe an upper-extremity joint MR imaging study: **73221** (without contrast), **73222** (with contrast), and **73223** (without followed by with contrast). Since "with contrast" MR arthrography was performed, the "with contrast" study code (**73222**) was selected.

CODING TIP

Fluoroscopy used for the intra-articular injection for enhanced (with contrast) MR arthrography and enhanced (with contrast) CT arthrography involves more physician work and a higher degree of complexity than the intravenous injection of contrast included with other MR or CT enhanced procedures. Therefore, if *no* radiographic arthrography procedure is performed in conjunction with an enhanced MR arthrography or enhanced CT arthrography, and fluoroscopic guidance is used for the enhanced MR or CT joint injection, it is appropriate to code **76003** (Fluoroscopic guidance for needle placement) separately. For example, if only shoulder MR imaging with contrast arthrography procedure is performed, it would be reported with CPT codes **23350** (Injection procedure for shoulder arthrography or enhanced CT/MRI shoulder arthrography), **76003** (Fluoroscopic guidance for needle placement), and **73222** (Magnetic resonance [eg, proton] imaging, any joint of upper extremity; with contrast material[s]).

EXERCISES 4, 5

Answer: (Exercise 4) **74160** Computed tomography, abdomen; with contrast material(s)

(Exercise 5) **72193** Computed tomography, pelvis; with contrast material(s)

CODING TIP

As noted in the Radiology section guidelines in the CPT codebook, the phrase "with contrast" used in the codes for procedures performed with contrast for imaging enhancement represents contrast material administered *intravascularly, intra-articularly, or intrathecally*. Note that oral and/or rectal contrast administration alone does not qualify as a study with contrast.

CODING TIP

Injection of intravascular contrast material is part of the "with contrast" CT, CT angiography, MR imaging, and MR angiography procedures and is not coded separately. However, injections of intra-articular and intrathecal contrast material are coded separately, eg, in the case of MR arthrography.

CODING TIP

High-osmolar contrast is included in the procedure code, whereas low-osmolar contrast may be coded separately, usually with a Healthcare Common Procedure Coding System (HCPCS) code, depending on the payment policies of the third-party payer.

Rationale for Code Selection

Selection of a CT study code is based on the anatomic site studied and whether contrast was used. In the scenario given, Omnipaque, a low-osmolar contrast agent, was power injected *intravenously* and a complete study of the abdomen and subsequently a complete study of the pelvis were performed; therefore, the "with contrast" CPT codes were chosen.

If a CT scan of the abdomen and one of the pelvis are performed on the same day, both procedures should be reported. Coding for only a CT of the abdomen would underestimate the additional work provided and resources used to examine the pelvis.

EXERCISE 6

Coding for Arterial Catheterization

Answer: **36246** Selective catheter placement, arterial system; initial second order abdominal, pelvic, or lower extremity artery branch, within a vascular family

75625 Aortography, abdominal, by serialography, radiological supervision and interpretation

75716 Angiography, extremity, bilateral, radiological supervision and interpretation

Coding for Stent Placement

Answer: **37205** Transcatheter placement of an intravascular stent(s), (non-coronary vessel), percutaneous; initial vessel

75960 Transcatheter introduction of intravascular stent(s), (non-coronary vessel), percutaneous and/or open, radiological supervision and interpretation, each vessel

Rationale for Code Selection

When coding for arterial catheterization, one should code for the highest-level catheterization performed in each vascular family and use the add-on "each additional vessel" code for additional catheterized vessel in each vascular family. In this case, the highest-level catheterization was of the right external iliac artery. From a left groin approach, this is a second-order catheterization (**36246**).

Although nonselective aortic catheterization was initially performed, the nonselective aortic catheterization code (**36200**) should not be used, as the operator went on and performed more selective catheterization (**36246**) from the same access. The work inherent in the nonselective catheterization (**36200**) has been included in the valuation of the higher-level selective catheterization code (**36246**).

For radiological supervision and interpretation of the diagnostic angiogram, one should code for each distinct named service performed. In this case, a complete angiographic evaluation of both the abdominal aorta (**75625**) and bilateral lower extremities (**75716**) was performed. Since runoff evaluation of the pelvis is inherent in a full and complete lower-extremity

Aortography
75600–75630

A radiographic contrast study is performed on the abdominal or thoracic aorta.

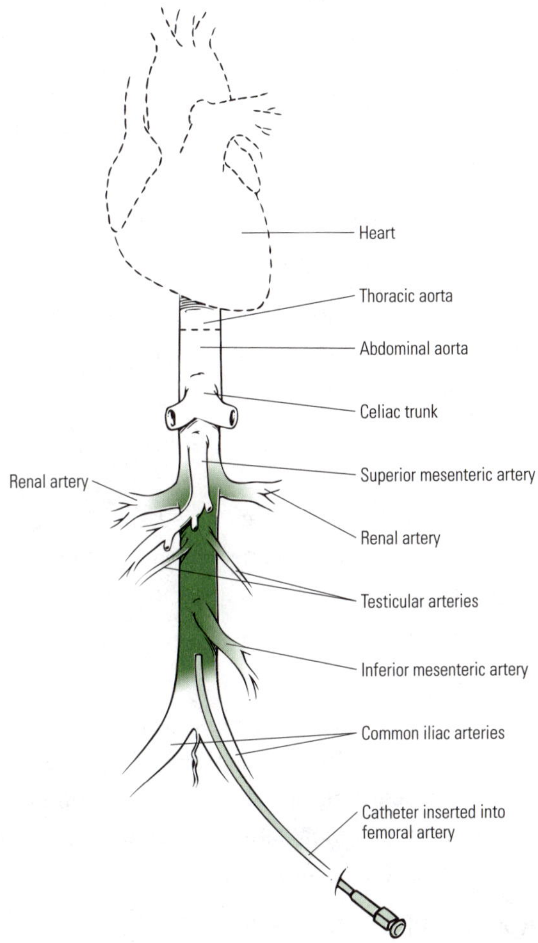

angiogram (**75716**) and was performed nonselectively, the use of the selective pelvic angiogram code (**75736**) is clearly not appropriate in this setting.

Balloon dilation should be coded as angioplasty only when it is performed with the intention of providing definitive treatment. Accordingly, predilation of a critical lesion, intended only to facilitate passage of a stent, is not separately coded as an iliac angioplasty procedure. Similarly, the use of an angioplasty balloon to optimize apposition of a stent to the vessel wall or facilitate dilation of an incompletely expanded stent should not be separately coded as an angioplasty procedure.

When an endovascular stent is placed, codes should be used to describe both the surgical procedure component itself (**37205**) and the appropriate radiological supervision and interpretation (**75960**). This includes additional imaging to facilitate stent placement and completion angiography. These imaging services should not be additionally coded. Therefore, in the scenario above, balloon angioplasty to assist in the placement of the stent and repeat angiography were not coded.

CODING TIP

It does not matter if multiple myocardial perfusion imaging (SPECT) studies are performed on the same date or on subsequent dates. The choice of the CPT code will remain the *multiple* study code (**78465**) and not the *single* study code (**78464**). A frequently asked question is whether code **78464** (myocardial perfusion imaging; tomographic [SPECT], single study at rest or stress [exercise and/or pharmacologic], with or without quantification) can be reported twice, once for each day. The answer is no. It does not matter if the myocardial perfusion studies are done on the same or different days.

CODING TIP

If a pharmacologic stress agent is used to perform a stress test, this should be reported separately by means of the appropriate agent HCPCS code, description, and number of units.

EXERCISE 7

Answer: **78465** Myocardial perfusion imaging; tomographic SPECT, multiple studies, at rest and/or stress (exercise and/or pharmacologic) and redistribution and/or rest injection, with or without quantification

+78478 Myocardial perfusion study with wall motion, qualitative or quantitative study (List separately in addition to code for primary procedure)

+78480 Myocardial perfusion study with ejection fraction (List separately in addition to code for primary procedure)

(One of the codes that follow should be chosen for the stress portion, on the basis of the facility's particular financial arrangement with physician and the setting.)

Physician Office Setting

93016 Cardiovascular stress test using maximal or submaximal treadmill or bicycle exercise, continuous electrocardiograph monitoring, and/or pharmacological stress; physician supervision only, without interpretation and report.

Hospital Outpatient Setting

93017-TC Cardiovascular stress test using maximal or submaximal treadmill or bicycle exercise, continuous electrocardiographic monitoring, and/or pharmacological stress; tracing only, without interpretation and report

Radiopharmaceutical Coding

1 unit **A9502** Supply of radiopharmaceutical diagnostic imaging agent, Technetium Tc99m Tetrofosmin, per unit dose

3 units **A9500** Supply of radiopharmaceutical diagnostic imaging agent, Thallous Chloride, per mCi

Rationale for Code Selection

Myocardial perfusion imaging is one of the most common nuclear medicine procedures performed, yet the codes to describe a typical complete procedure can be complex. Key words that led to the proper selection of codes in this case are as follows:

SPECT: Nuclear medicine procedures can be performed by planar imaging or SPECT. Basically, planar imaging is a two-dimensional image, while SPECT (single photon emission computed tomography) is a three-dimensional image.

Gated: Gating during a myocardial perfusion study is the use of electrocardiography to gather a series of images related to the patient's electrocardiogram. The additional information obtained is described in the two add-on codes below.

Ejection Fraction: Obtained by gating a myocardial perfusion imaging study, ejection fraction is reported as a percentage of the resting or diastolic left ventricular volume that is ejected with each beat of the heart. This is reported by the add-on code **78480**.

Wall Motion: Obtained by gating a myocardial perfusion imaging study, wall motion is the study of the movement of the heart muscle; this can be with a reported number (quantitative) or upon visual review (qualitative). Wall motion is reported by the add-on code **78478**.

Stress and Rest: The mention of both a stress and a rest study indicates that two myocardial perfusion imaging procedures were performed; when two or more such procedures are performed, the proper choice of code is "multiple studies."

Stress Test: The key elements in selecting the proper code for a stress test are as follows:

- Who supervised the study
- What relationship that supervisor has to the facility
- Who interpreted and reported the stress test study

Knowing the answers to these elements will lead to the proper CPT code.

In this case, the nuclear medicine physician did not interpret or report the tracing, and the setting or exact financial relationship between the nuclear medicine physician and the facility is unknown. There are two options. The proper code should be chosen when this relationship information is obtained.

In any stress test, the method selected to accomplish the stress will not change the code (eg, whether an exercise stress test is performed on a treadmill or a pharmacological stress agent such as adenosine or dipyridamole is used). Only the elements listed above will have a bearing on which CPT code to select.

CODING TIP

When multiple procedures, other than E/M services, are performed at the same session by the same provider, the primary procedure or service may be reported as listed. The additional procedure(s) or service(s) may be identified by appending the modifier 51 to the additional procedure or service code(s). This modifier should not be appended to designated nuclear medicine "add-on" codes such as **78020**, **78478**, **78480**, and **78496**.

EXERCISE 8

Answer: **78320** Bone and/or joint imaging; tomographic (SPECT)

78306-51 Bone and/or joint imaging; whole body

Radiopharmaceutical Coding

A9503 Supply of radiopharmaceutical diagnostic imaging agent, Technetium Tc99m Medronate, per dose, up to 30 mCi

Rationale for Code Selection

In general, for nuclear medicine bone scan imaging, the top of the head to below the knees is considered whole-body imaging. Because of the lower back pain, a SPECT image of the lumbar spine was also performed in this example. The primary code in this combination would be the SPECT code. Modifier 51 is appended to the whole-body procedure code.

A separate code (charge) is submitted for the radiopharmaceutical used. Some payers may ask for an invoice for radiopharmaceuticals that are reported.

CODING TIP

The only acceptable bone scan code pair combination is **78320** and **78306**. If alternate procedures are performed during a bone scan, such as limited areas, multiple areas, or three-phase study, plus a SPECT study, then only one of the procedures is reported. The code reporting the single procedure with the highest level of work performed should be selected. For example, if a multiple-body-area scan and SPECT were performed, only the SPECT would be reported. If a three-phase bone study and SPECT were performed, only the three-phase study would be reported.

Chapter 5

Medicine Answers

Contact Lens Services

EXERCISE 1

Answer: **92310** Prescription of optical and physical characteristics of and fitting of contact lenses, with medical supervision of adaptation; corneal lens, both eyes, except for aphakia

Report the appropriate established code from E/M codes, or General Ophthalmologic Services code

92015 Determination of refractive state

76514 Ophthalmic ultrasound, echography, diagnostic; corneal pachymetry, unilateral or bilateral (determination of corneal thickness)

(HCPCS) **V2510-RT** Contact lens, gas permeable, spherical, per lens

(HCPCS) **V2510-LT** Contact lens, gas permeable, spherical, per lens

Rationale for Code Selection

Code **92310** is used to report the professional services provided to properly fit the eye with the appropriate contact lenses. This can include the supply of the materials or can be reported without the materials. This service is for patients who either have not had cataract surgery at all or have had cataract surgery with the placement of an intraocular lens. For this purpose, only patients without their physiologic lens and without an intraocular lens are considered aphakic.

Code **92015** is a special ophthalmological service and is separately reported. Special ophthalmological services may be reported in addition to the general ophthalmological services or E/M services. Code **92015** is intended to represent a bilateral procedure or service. It is not appropriate to report **92015** per eye. It is also not appropriate to use modifier 50 (or the RT or LT HCPCS designation) when this code is reported. If refractive state is determined on one eye, then modifier 52 should be appended to the code to indicate reduced services.

There is no mandate that the ophthalmology codes must be used instead of the E/M codes. As stated in the instructions for use of CPT, the physician should report the code(s) that most accurately identifies the service(s) or procedure(s) performed. It is important to note that the general ophthalmological service codes **92002**, **92004**, **92012**, and **92014** are specific to the typical services rendered during an ophthalmological visit. However, the code that most accurately identifies the service performed should be reported, whether it be an E/M service code or an ophthalmology visit code.

The CPT coding guidelines stated in *Principles of CPT® Coding, Third Edition* (AMA Press, 2003) indicate that corneal topography is considered an inherent part of the visit code and is therefore not reported separately. However, reporting requirements for corneal topography and the supply of lens material may vary among third-party payers. It is important to contact the appropriate third-party payer for its specific reporting requirements for corneal topography and supply of lens material.

CPT code **76514** (ophthalmic ultrasound, pachymetry) is used to determine corneal thickness. It is indicated for patients with corneal disease when the central corneal thickness is potentially affected. Corneal thickness in this case can be an indirect indicator of the progression of the disease.

EXERCISE 2

Answer: **92311** Prescription of optical and physical characteristics of and fitting of contact lenses, with medical supervision of adaptation; corneal lens, for aphakia, one eye

Report appropriate initial consultation code

92015 Determination of refractive state

76514 Ophthalmic ultrasound, echography, diagnostic; corneal pachymetry, unilateral or bilateral (determination of corneal thickness)

(HCPCS) **V2599-RT** supply of an aphakic contact lens for right eye

(HCPCS) **V2020** Frame

(HCPCS) **V2300-RT** Trifocal lens for right eye

(HCPCS) **V2799-RT** Deluxe lens for right eye materials (Progressive lens)

(HCPCS) **V2100-LT** Single vision lens for left eye

Rationale for Code Selection

Code **92311** is reported because the patient has aphakia in one eye, as a result of physiologic lens extraction. Aphakia is not the diagnosis if an intraocular lens has been placed in the eye.

The use of contact lenses is medically necessary in unilateral aphakia because of the high degree of aneisometropia and resultant loss of binocularity without contact lenses.

Since code **76514** indicates unilateral or bilateral, it can be reported for one or both eyes.

The CPT coding guidelines stated in *Principles of CPT® Coding, Third Edition* (AMA Press, 2003) indicate that corneal topography is considered an inherent part of the visit code and is therefore not reported separately. However, reporting requirements for corneal topography and the supply of lens material may vary among third-party payers. It is important to contact the appropriate third-party payer for its specific reporting requirements for corneal topography and supply of lens material

Spectacle Services

EXERCISE 1

Answer: Report either **99214** or **92014**

92015 Determination of refractive state

92354 Fitting of spectacle-mounted low-vision aid; single element system

Rationale for Code Selection

Code **92354** is reported for the magnification device selected, which is a spectacle-mounted, single-element (bifocal segment) prescription.

Code **92015** (refraction) should be reported as a distinct service. In low-vision care, trial frame refraction is a more complex refraction. Code **92015** is a special ophthalmological service and is separately reported. Code **92015** is intended to represent a bilateral procedure or service. It is not appropriate to report **92015** per eye. It is also not appropriate to use modifier 50 (or the RT or LT HCPCS designation) when this code is reported. If refractive state is determined on one eye, then modifier 52 should be appended to the code to indicate reduced services.

Special ophthalmological services may be reported in addition to the general ophthalmological services or E/M services. There is no mandate that the ophthalmology codes must be used instead of the E/M codes. As stated in the instructions for use of CPT, the physician should report the code(s) that most accurately identifies the service(s) or procedure(s) performed. It is important to note that the general ophthalmological service codes **92002**, **92004**, **92012**, and **92014** are specific to the typical services rendered during an ophthalmological visit. However, the code that most accurately identifies the service performed should be reported, whether it be an E/M service code or an ophthalmology visit code.

EXERCISE 2

Answer: **92355** Fitting of spectacle mounted low vision aid; telescopic or other compound lens system

99205 Office or other outpatient visit (extensive evaluation and counseling are required to fully prepare this patient for use of bioptic devices, especially for driving)
(Alternative coding would be with modifier 21 Prolonged Evaluation and Management Services, with code **92004**)

92015 Determination of refractive state

97530 Therapeutic activities, direct (one-on-one) patient contact by the provider (use of dynamic activities to improve functional performance), each 15 minutes

Rationale for Code Selection

Code **92355** is reported for the telescope mounted as bioptic for driving (compound lens system).

Code **92015** (refraction) should be reported as a distinct service. In low-vision care, trial frame refraction is a more complex refraction. Code **92015** is a special ophthalmological service and is separately reported. Special ophthalmological services may be reported in addition to the general ophthalmological services or E/M services. Code **92015** is intended to represent a bilateral procedure or service. It is not appropriate to report **92015** per eye. It is also not appropriate to use modifier 50 (or the RT or LT HCPCS designation) when this code is reported. If refractive state is determined on one eye, then modifier 52 should be appended to the code to indicate reduced services.

Code **99205** is reported for low-vision evaluation done to determine the ocular health and functional vision status. Depending on examination elements, case complexity, and duration of counseling, other code options would be **99203** and **99204** or **92002**.

The appropriate Physical Therapy and Rehabilitation code (eg, code **97530**) is reported for providing instruction in the proper uses of a bioptic for driving. The physician or an employee of the physician may provide the recommended follow-up incident to the physician's professional services, and follow-up must be provided under the physician's direct personal supervision. The **97000** codes are primarily used by occupational and physical therapy providers but are considered appropriate for "incident to" care provided by physicians. One or several units (15-minute periods) can be billed when properly documented. Third-party payers should be contacted for their reporting requirements for low-vision instruction and counseling.

Special Otorhinolaryngologic Services

EXERCISE 1

Answer: A

92610 Evaluation of oral and pharyngeal swallowing function

Rationale for Code Selection

Codes **92610**, **92611**, and **92612** describe different evaluations of swallowing function. Code **92611** describes the use of fluoroscopy to evaluate the swallowing function. Code **92612** describes the use of a flexible fiberoptic endoscope to evaluate the swallowing function within the pharynx and larynx. Code **92610** does not include the use of fluoroscopy or a flexible fiberoptic endoscope to evaluate the swallowing function. Since the example evaluated the swallowing function without the use of fluoroscopy or flexible fiberoptic endoscope, the appropriate code to report the evaluation of the swallowing function is code **92610**.

EXERCISE 2

Answer: **92612** Flexible fiberoptic endoscopic evaluation of swallowing by cine or video recording

92613 physician interpretation and report only

Rationale for Code Selection

The physician performing the study would report both codes **92612** and **92613** because he performed the entire study as well as providing an interpretation with written report.

Allergy and Clinical Immunology

EXERCISE 1

Answer: 95004 Percutaneous tests (scratch, puncture, prick) with allergenic extracts, immediate type reaction, specify number of tests

Rationale for Code Selection

When a patient is suspected to have an immediate hypersensitivity (IgE-mediated) reaction to an inhalant or food allergen, code **95004** is reported for percutaneous testing to confirm a clinically suspected sensitivity and to rule out sensitivities.

EXERCISE 2

Answer: 95010 Percutaneous tests (scratch, puncture, prick) sequential and incremental, with drugs, biologicals or venoms, immediate type reaction, specify number of tests

95015 Intracutaneous (intradermal) tests, sequential and incremental, with drugs, biologicals, or venoms, immediate type reaction, specify number of tests

Rationale for Code Selection

Codes **95010** and **95015** are distinguished from **95004** and **95024** in that they are used for drugs, biologics, and venoms, which involve more individualized preparation and more careful monitoring and decision making by the physician and nurse.

EXERCISE 3

Answer: 95024 Intracutaneous (intradermal) tests with allergenic extracts, immediate type reaction, specify number of tests

Rationale for Code Selection

This code is reported when a patient is suspected to have an immediate hypersensitivity (IgE-mediated) reaction to an inhalant allergen and has a negative percutaneous test. An intracutaneous test is more sensitive, so it may detect the presence of specific IgE when a percutaneous test is negative. An intracutaneous test should not be performed unless a corresponding percutaneous test has been performed for that allergen and is negative.

EXERCISE 4

Answer: 94070 Prolonged postexposure evaluation of bronchospasm with multiple spirometric determinations after antigen, cold air, methacholine or other chemical agent, with subsequent spirometrics

95070 Inhalation bronchial challenge testing (not including necessary pulmonary function tests); with histamine, methacholine, or similar compounds

Rationale for Code Selection

This code is reported when the differential diagnosis includes asthma or airway hyperreactivity, and testing beyond airway reversibility is needed to make a diagnosis or determine severity of hyperreactivity.

This code is commonly reported with **94070**. A J code for the substance (methacholine, etc) used in the challenge may also be included. These two codes must be reported together because one is the inhalation challenge and one is measuring the airflow.

EXERCISE 5

Answer: 95180 Rapid desensitization procedure, each hour (eg, insulin, penicillin, equine serum)

Rationale for Code Selection

This code may also be used for rapid desensitization to other allergens, and prior authorization may be helpful if the procedure is done on an elective basis.

Since this is a time-based code, documentation should include the results of the monitoring and observation done during the desensitization and the claim form should have the hours of the actual desensitization procedure in the units.

For penicillin, skin testing must be done before desensitization to determine safe starting dose and/or need for desensitization.

Neurostimulators, Analysis-Programming

EXERCISE 1

Answer: 95978 Electronic analysis of implanted neurostimulator pulse generator system (eg, rate, pulse amplitude and duration, battery status, electrode selectability and polarity, impedance and patient compliance measurements), complex deep brain neurostimulator pulse generator/transmitter, with initial or subsequent programming; first hour

+95979 Each additional 30 minutes after first hour (List separately in addition to code for primary procedure)

Report the service as one unit of **95978**, four units of **95979**.

Rationale for Code Selection

Communication with the patient, family, and other health care professionals (including written and telephone reports and orders) on the day of the analysis are considered part of the postoperative work for this procedure. It is important to carefully document in the patient's medical record all adjustments made to the stimulation parameters and ongoing device operation.

Codes **95978** and **95979** are used for programming with a "complex" brain neurostimulation system. In essence, such a system consists of the following: two "four-contact" leads (thus, eight total electrical contacts); a single "eight-contact" lead; or two "eight contact" leads (thus 16 total electrical contacts). The number of possible electrode combinations for polarity and use ranges from over 100,000 to about 60 million, depending upon which of these three systems are used. Furthermore, many of the Food and Drug Administration (FDA)-approved "complex" systems allow three to four different combinations to be used at the same time thus increasing the possible stimulation settings by a factor of 3 to 10 times. Code **95978** refers to the initial 60 minutes of programming for a complex neurostimulation system. Code **95979** refers to an additional 30 minutes of programming for a complex neurostimulation system. When separately identifiable evaluation and management services are provided, they are coded separately. The time included in the evaluation and management service is exclusive of any time used to determine the coding of **95978** and **95979**.

Health and Behavior Assessment/Intervention

EXERCISE 1

Answer: False

Rationale for Code Selection

These codes may be reported by, but are not limited to, psychologists, advanced practice nurses, clinical social workers, and other nonphysician health care professionals within their scope of practice who have specialty or subspecialty training in health and behavior assessment/intervention procedures. These codes are *not* intended to be used by physicians. Instead, physicians performing these services may identify their efforts by choosing the E/M codes appropriate to the type and level of service being provided.

EXERCISE 2

Answer: **96150** Health and behavior assessment (eg, health-focused clinical interview, behavioral observations, psychophysiological monitoring, health-oriented questionnaires), each 15 minutes face-to-face with the patient; initial assessment

Rationale for Code Selection

Code **96150** is reported because the patient was assessed by means of a standardized questionnaire and the administration of various health and behavior assessment instruments.

EXERCISE 3

Answer: 96155 Health and behavior intervention, each 15 minutes, face-to-face; family (without the patient present)

Rationale for Code Selection

Since the patient was unable to travel to the sessions between hospitalizations, the patient's wife saw the health care provider for training in how to assist the patient in objectively monitoring his pain and in applying exercises learned via his treatment sessions to manage pain. Therefore, the appropriate code to report for this scenario is **96155**.

Physical Medicine and Rehabilitation

EXERCISE 1

Answer: 97001 Physical therapy evaluation

97014 Application of a modality to one or more areas; electrical stimulation (unattended) (1 unit)

97012 traction, mechanical (1 unit)

97140 Manual therapy techniques (eg, mobilization/manipulation, manual lymphatic drainage, manual traction), one or more regions, each 15 minutes (2 units)

97535 Self-care/home management training (eg, activities of daily living (ADL), and compensatory training, meal preparation, safety procedures, and instructions in use of assistive technology devices/adaptive equipment) direct one-on-one contact by provider, each 15 minutes (1 unit)

> **CODING TIP**
>
> The appropriate discrimination between **97535** and **97537** should be based on the desired outcome of treatment and its application to the home or work/community environment. Documentation should support that this is a distinct procedural service.

Rationale for Code Selection

Code **97001** is used because a physical therapist must perform a comprehensive evaluation at the time of the first visit. This is not a time-based code and should be reported once per episode, regardless of how many body parts are involved.

Code **97014** is reported because the patient received unattended electrical stimulation to the cervical and lumbar spine for 15 minutes each. This code can be reported only once or as one unit per session, regardless of the number of body parts being treated, because the narrative of the code states "application of a modality to one or more areas."

Code **97012** indicates that the patient received 15 minutes of mechanical traction to the cervical spine. This code can be reported only once or as one unit per session, regardless of the number of body parts being treated, because the narrative of the code states "application of a modality to one or more areas." Also, this is not a time-based code.

Treatment of the patient with soft-tissue mobilization to the cervical, thoracic, and lumbar spine for an aggregate time of 25 minutes is reported with code **97140**. This is a time-based code (15 minutes per unit). Code **97140** should be reported with two units for the procedure. Coding should not be determined on the basis of the number of minutes spent per body part but rather the total aggregate time.

Code **97535** is reported because the therapist devoted a separate and distinct procedural service to the patient for the purpose of instruction in managing the injury at home and preventing secondary injury.

> **CODING TIP**
>
> Soft-tissue mobilization is just one of many possible techniques considered to be covered under the manual therapy code (**97140**).

EXERCISE 2

Answer: **97110** Therapeutic procedure, one or more areas, each 15 minutes; therapeutic exercises to develop strength and endurance, range of motion and flexibility (Report twice or as 2 units)

97140 Manual therapy techniques (eg, mobilization/manipulation, manual lymphatic drainage, manual traction), one or more regions, each 15 minutes (Report once or as 1 unit)

97116 Therapeutic procedure, one or more areas, each 15 minutes; gait training (includes stair climbing) (Report once or as 1 unit)

> **CODING TIP**
>
> Therapeutic exercise (**97110**) includes exercises to develop flexibility (sometimes noted as passive and active range of motion), strength, and endurance.

Rationale for Code Selection

The therapist provided 30 minutes of instruction in exercises to increase joint range of motion as well as strengthening exercises. Code **97110** is a 15-minute code. Therefore, it is appropriate to report it with 2 units.

It is appropriate to report manual therapy for the soft-tissue mobilization procedure used to decrease scar adherence with code **97140.** Ten minutes of soft-tissue mobilization should be reported once or as one unit, since this is a 15-minute time-based code.

Fitting for and instruction in use of a new assistive device for ambulation on any and all surfaces should be reported as gait training with code **97116.** This is a timed code, and it is appropriate to report it using one unit.

> **CODING TIP**
>
> The documentation must reflect that skilled care was provided during the time billed as gait training (**97116**). Supervised ambulation without delivery of skilled care is not considered gait training.

EXERCISE 3

Answer: **97150** Therapeutic procedure(s), group (2 or more individuals)

Rationale for Code Selection

If a therapist provides skilled intervention in a group setting with direct contact, the time spent with each patient in the group is coded as **97150.** This is not a timed-based code.

> **CODING TIP**
>
> Group therapy (**97150**) can be reported only once per patient per visit.

EXERCISE 4

Answer: **97750** Physical performance test or measurement (eg, musculoskeletal, functional capacity), with written report, each 15 minutes (Report as 16 units)

Rationale for Code Selection

Code **97550** for physical performance testing is used when the provider evaluates performance related to specific tasks. This is a time-based code, 15 minutes per unit. Multiple units can be reported at each visit.

Medical Nutrition Therapy

EXERCISE 1

Answer: 97802 Medical nutrition therapy; initial assessment and intervention, individual, face-to-face with the patient, each 15 minutes

EXERCISE 2

Answer: 97803 Medical nutrition therapy; re-assessment and intervention, individual, face-to-face with the patient, each 15 minutes

G0270 MNT, re-assessment and subsequent intervention(s) following second referral in same year for change in diagnosis, medical condition, or treatment regimen (including additional hours needed for renal disease), individual, face-to-face with the patient, each 15 minutes.

EXERCISE 3

Answer: 97804 Medical nutrition therapy; group (2 or more individual[s]), each 30 minutes

G0271 MNT re-assessment and subsequent intervention(s), following second referral in same year for change in diagnosis, medical condition, or treatment regimen (including additional hours needed for renal disease), group (2 or more individuals), each 30 minutes

Rationale for Code Selection (Exercises 1–3)

The initial MNT visit is always reported with MNT CPT code **97802**. Subsequent visits are coded with **97803** if individual, one-on-one MNT services are provided, or **97804** if the patient receives MNT services in a group (two or more individuals). On the basis of the RD's critical thinking and decision making, and interaction with the patient, the RD determines whether follow-up MNT services will be provided in group sessions instead of through individual sessions. This determines follow-up MNT CPT code selection.

For Medicare-covered MNT services, after three hours of MNT services, and when additional hours of MNT services in one calendar year are medically necessary, RDs use **G0270** for subsequent individual, one-on-one MNT services, or **G0271** for group MNT services.

CCODING TIP

For Medicare patients with diabetes and nondialysis kidney disease, who often require additional individual MNT beyond 3 hours in one calendar year, MNT code G0270 is reported instead of MNT CPT code **97803**.

CODING TIP

For Medicare patients with diabetes and nondialysis kidney disease, who often require additional group MNT beyond 3 hours in one calendar year, MNT code G0271 is used instead of MNT CPT code **97804**.

CODING TIP

Although all MNT CPT codes are time based, group MNT (**97804**) is provided in 30-minute units compared with 15-minute units for MNT initial assessment and intervention (**97802**) and MNT reassessment and intervention (**97803**).

CODING TIP

Initial MNT assessment and intervention (**97802**) always precedes use of the group MNT CPT code (**97804**).

Osteopathic and Chiropractic Manipulative Treatment

EXERCISE 1

Answer: 98940 Chiropractic manipulative treatment (CMT); spinal, one to two regions

CODING TIP

When MNT services are performed for home healthcare patients, code **97802** or **97803** is reported instead of Home Health Procedures/ Services code **99509**, home visit for assistance with activities of daily living and personal care.

Rationale for Code Selection

The CMT codes are reported according the region(s) manipulated. The five spinal regions are cervical (includes atlanto-occipital joint), thoracic (includes costovertebral and costotransverse joints), lumbar, sacral, and pelvic (sacroiliac joint). Since the C2 cervical region and L4 and L5 lumbar segments were manipulated, only code **98940** should be reported to reflect the two regions.

EXERCISE 2

Answer: 98943 Chiropractic manipulative treatment (CMT); extraspinal, one or more regions

Rationale for Code Selection

The five extraspinal regions are the head (including temporomandibular joint, excluding the atlanto-occipital region), lower extremities, upper extremities, rib cage (excluding costotransverse and costovertebral joints), and abdomen. Code **98943** should be reported for manipulation of the extraspinal regions of the elbow, hand, and wrist.

Index

A

B

C

D

E

F

G

H

I

K

L

M

N

O

P

CPT Codes Cited

Code ranges (eg, **00100–01999**) indicate reference to the entire code range, not to individual codes within that range.